"Within these pages Archbishop Daniel Williams has presented a clear, lucid and prophetic call to the Body of Christ at large and to leaders in particular. In a very personal way he takes us on a journey of discovery of some key elements, often overlooked by many in certain portions of the Lord's one Church, that are necessary for the fulfillment of the Great Commission and the unity of God's people. There is a clarion call here for the streams of the Church to find their divine source as one river again that the saving purposes of God for the nations and peoples of the earth may be fulfilled in Christ. I am very expectant about the ways in which our sovereign Lord and Savior will use this effort to speak deeply to the hearts of many across all the streams of the Church in our day."

> *P. Wayne Boosahda*
> *Presiding Bishop of the Communion of Convergence Churches, USA,*
> *a Province of CEEC*
> *Archdiocese of St. Patrick*
> *Franklin*

"Bishop Williams has produced a wonderful and insightful text on the convergence movement. It brings clarity, Biblical insights and balance into a movement that has not yet fulfilled its God ordained destiny. *The Sound of Rushing Waters* is based on Bishop Williams' decades of commitment to and experiences in the convergence movement. I believe this work will be an indispensable tool for pastors and lay leaders who wish to participate in this inspired movement to bring the church to its full potential."

> *William L. DeArteaga*
> *Hispanic Pastor, Light of Christ Anglican Church*
> *Marietta*

"*The Sound of Rushing Waters* uncovers a vein of gold to help us understand the valid Biblical wealth within the convergence/apostolic movements. Balance comes from sound exposition of the Word, insightful historical interpretation and relevant application to our 21st century context. Daniel blends these three veins of understanding into a balanced approach that will help provide unity to the global Great Commission community."

> *Howard Foltz*
> *Founder and President, AIMS*
> *Professor, Global Evangelization, Regent University*
> *Virginia Beach*

"Daniel Williams is a clear-minded thinker and a sensitive spiritual leader. We could use more of these! Thanks, Dan, for providing the insights you have in *The Sound of Rushing Waters*."

> *Jack W. Hayford, Chancellor*
> *The King's College and Seminary*
> *Los Angeles*

D0684371

"I am thrilled that in *The Sound of Rushing Waters* Bishop Daniel Williams has issued a clarion call for a divided Christianity to take seriously our Lord's desire that we be one, as He and the Father are one. He sees a critical element of the recovery to be founded upon the recovery of an authentic apostolic and historic Episcopate that takes itself and the future of unity more seriously than has been evidenced in most ecclesiastical institutions. But the Church is more than an institution, and the Holy Spirit is alive and well, inviting faithful leaders to revisit their roots and imagine their future. Building on his vision, his broad personal experience, and his current successes in the convergence movements of our day, so strongly lived out at Christ the Redeemer, in Ponte Vedra Beach, FL, Williams makes his case that a new Reformation is well underway. He and his people are living it."

Stephen Jecko
The Rt. Rev. Stephen H. Jecko, D.Min, D.D.
(Seventh Bishop of the Episcopal Diocese of Florida, retired; former member of the Standing Commission on Ecumenical Relations of the Episcopal Church; currently serving as Assisting Bishop of the Episcopal Diocese of Dallas, and a Suffragan Bishop of the Network of Anglican Communion Dioceses and Parishes)

"Those of us who delight in hearing what the Spirit is saying to the churches today frequently overlook what the Spirit has been saying to the churches yesterday. *The Sound of Rushing Waters* helps greatly to correct this weakness. Daniel Williams does a superb job of relating the contemporary moves of God to their vital historical context. I strongly recommend that church leaders read this enlightening book."

C. Peter Wagner, Presiding Apostle
International Coalition of Apostles
Global Harvest Ministries
Chancellor, Wagner Leadership Institute
Colorado Springs

"*The Sound of Rushing Waters* is biblical, historical, theological and practical. The future of the church is not found in a new radical and innovative start, but is rooted in the great traditions now converging. Thanks to Archbishop Daniel Williams for showing us the convergence through which God is bringing deeper unity to his people."

Robert E. Webber, Th.D.
Myers Professor of Ministry, Northern Seminary
Director, Institute of Worship Studies
Wheaton

DANIEL W. WILLIAMS

The Sound of
RUSHING
WATERS

A prophetic call to embrace the Great Commandment
in order to fulfill the Great Commission

Dquest

Destiny Quest Publications
A Division of Dquest Group, Incorporated
P.O. Box 52
Ponte Vedra Beach, Florida 32004-0052
www.dquestgroup.com

The Sound of Rushing Waters
Copyright ©2005 Daniel W. Williams
All rights reserved

Cover Design by Alpha Advertising
Interior Design by Pine Hill Graphics

Destiny Quest Publications
A Division of Dquest Group, Incorporated
P.O. Box 52
Ponte Vedra Beach, Florida 32004-0052
www.dquestgroup.com

Library of Congress Cataloging-in-Publication Data
(Provided by Cassidy Cataloguing Services, Inc.)

Williams, Daniel W.
    The sound of rushing waters : a prophetic call to embrace the great commandment in order to fulfill the Great Commission / Daniel W. Williams. -- 1st ed. -- Ozark, AL : ACW Press, 2005.

    p. ; cm.

    Includes bibliographical references.
    ISBN: 1-932124-66-7
    ISBN-13: 978-1-932124-66-8

    1. Great Commission (Bible) 2. Church--Unity. 3. Christian union. 4. Christianity. I. Title.

BV2074 .W55 2005
266--dc22   0509

Printed in the United States of America.

This book is dedicated to all those who through direct relationships or their distant inspiration helped form me as a man and as a minister.

This book is dedicated to all who may be helped in their formation by it.

This book is dedicated to the Church, the gloriously diverse and eternally blessed Bride of Christ.

This book is dedicated to the fulfillment of the Great Commandment and the Great Commission in this generation.

Foreword

—◦◦◦◦—

In John 17 the high priestly prayer of Jesus to His Father was that we might be one. The intent and purpose of unity is to produce a tangible witness to the world.

The Lord in every generation picks men and women to lead the Body of Christ into new waters of understanding. Bishop Daniel Williams is such a man chosen by God to bring a message of "convergence" to a post-reformation, fragmented Body of Christ in the twenty-first century.

I believe Daniel has heard the voice of God, and in this book he clearly and concisely conveys the vision of Biblical unity for the purpose of finishing the Great Commission. Daniel not only uses heuristic theology (raising issues that require ongoing discussion), but also traverses the three streams of the church, passionately pioneering a path through the theological prejudices to the river of God. There is a second reformation in action and Daniel has sounded a clarion call.

I highly recommend this book for all Christians, pastors and students of God's Word.

Daniel, I am honored to know you as a friend and colleague. Thank you for your integrity, courage and passion in writing this book. I hear the sound.

God bless,
Bishop Van Gayton

Contents

———❧———

Introduction 15

1. Journey and Formation 21
2. Unity with Purpose 42
3. The People of God 51
4. The Church Universal 66
5. The Apostolic Church 86
6. Structural Challenges of the Modern Church 107
7. Future Church 124
8. The Roles of Bishops in the Contemporary Church . . 139
9. Road Map to the Finish Line. 171

Appendices:
    I: Additional Information
       on the Author's Journey 188
    II: The Primary Creeds. 196
    III: Common Elements of
        Convergence Churches 199
    IV: The Chicago-Lambeth Quadrilateral,
        1886 and 1888. 200
    V: The Lausanne Covenant, 1974 203

Bibliography 213

Preface

I have known Daniel Williams for many years, and together we have tackled the challenge of world missions around the globe. Now, in his powerful new book, Daniel presents to the Church—leadership and laity...denominations and independents alike—the necessity of embracing and facilitating a "New Reformation."

With all the skill of a learned scholar and the gentleness of an apostolic father, Daniel admonishes the Church Universal to lay aside our prejudices...our judgmentalism...even our denominational isolation and insulation...to accept God's challenge of unity with the same fervor and commitment as we have given the commandment to "Go into all the world to preach the gospel." In fact, Daniel suggests, it will only be through a renewed commitment to unity that we will be able to subjugate duplication and mixed messages on foreign fields to complete the Great Commission in these last days.

No matter what your religious background, Daniel has something important to say to you. He begins at the end in a scene from Revelation 19, where the voices of the redeemed throng of the ages rise in thunderous praise to God "like the sound of rushing waters"; and he asks, If there, why not here? Building upon that heavenly model, Daniel confronts us with the raw truth that God has always expected—and Jesus even commanded—unity among His people; that while being distinct in faith and practice is honoring to the Creator of diversity, we must do so without division or divorce.

Replete with memorable phrases, concise summaries of relevant church history, and rich with supporting Scripture, *The Sound of Rushing Waters* is guaranteed a long shelf life in your personal library. Daniel is bold enough—and kind enough—to tackle today's tough topics: the apostolic movement, the often-confused roles of prophets, pastors, elders and bishops, and bring them all into perspective with regard to the topic of unity. He discusses clerical ritual and rank, the new rise in "affinity" groups; and provides clear commentary on the church as part of corporate America, and on the current role of Christian media and the Information Age.

I highly recommend this insightful book as a wonderful resource for personal thought and study. Its clear chapter divisions and carefully footnoted quotes from both historical and contemporary sources provide a number of valuable springboards for ongoing exploration and confirmation of the topic. And by providing Key Discussion Points and Questions at each chapter's end, author Daniel Williams makes *The Sound of Rushing Waters* a tremendous tool for ministry staff or small group study.

If you need a renewed vision of what the Church can be—what it must be and will be—I encourage you to begin a personal journey through these pages. And I am sure that you will soon begin to hear, as I did, "the sound of rushing waters."

Charles E. Blair, Th.B., D.D., Litt.D.
Blair Foundation
Denver

Acknowledgments

———∽∾∿∽———

This book is a result of the labors, prayers, counsel and encouragement of many people. Please know that I am eternally grateful to each and every one.

I want to especially thank my indispensable assistant Robin Sheffield for her unceasing dedication to this project.

Special thanks go to those who helped develop and edit this work such as Patty Lurz, Kate Hendrickson, Debra Coram, Tim Frazier, William De Arteaga and especially my primary editor, Greg Bailey.

My deepest thanks to the staff, leadership and congregation of Christ the Redeemer Church for their encouragement and patience as they endured this project.

My fullest gratitude to the men and women who helped form me, especially to all of my mentors, spiritual parents, ministry colleagues, and to the multitude of historical and contemporary heroes of the faith that have taught and inspired my life and ministry.

Finally, but most importantly, I thank my wife Sharon— mother of our four children, grandmother of our five grandchildren, anointed minister, loving partner, companion, counselor and very best friend.

Introduction

———∞∞∞———

Then I heard what sounded like a great multitude, like the
roar of rushing waters and like loud peals of thunder,
shouting: 'Hallelujah! For our LORD God Almighty reigns. Let
us rejoice and be glad and give him glory! For the wedding of
the Lamb has come, and his bride has made herself ready.'"[1]
These awe-inspiring words declare the predetermined future
of the church. God will gather His bride *"from every nation,
tribe, people and language"*[2] into one unified community of
praise. There in the New Jerusalem, the heavenly city, believers
in Jesus from every generation and every divergent stream of
the church will flow into a river of praise and adoration of the
Lamb. All dissension will disappear and true, unmitigated
unity will prevail. The streams of the church that have flowed
distinct from one another upon the earth will combine to form
the mighty, roaring river that was prophetically announced by
King David: *"There is a river whose streams make glad the city
of God, the holy place where the Most High dwells."*[3] We will
most certainly hear the sound of rushing waters in that great
river. If you listen carefully, you can hear the torrents beginning to resound even now.

What then is the sound of rushing waters? It is the sound of
roaring praise to the Lamb as the church's collective voice is
commingled with the voices of angels and archangels and all of
the company of heaven. It is the thunderous sound of glorious
unity as the streams of faith flow together in ultimate fulfillment

---

1. Revelation 19:6-7.
2. Revelation 7:9.
3. Psalm 46:4.

of Jesus' prayer for our oneness. It is the sound of a victory shout as the redeemed of the Lord from every generation and from the whole earth celebrate the completion of the Great Commission.

As the last days of the church's earthly work approach, it is my belief that, for the sake of finishing the task, there will be a significant increase of visible unity in the body of Christ. Forgiveness, understanding and commitment will be required. Fresh models for unity and cooperation must emerge. Thankfully, there are many signs that this is precisely what is happening. One significant example is a growing phenomenon around the world in which the differing expressions of Christ's church are embracing uncharacteristic forms of worship and doctrine. Some have coined the term "The Convergence Movement"[4] to describe this occurrence. The Convergence Movement is not an abandonment of any of the historical streams, but a converging of each into a blended, contemporary expression. It is not so much a reaction to anything as a journey toward something. Perhaps we are in the midst of a *new* "reformation" that will prepare us for the end-time harvest.

Convergence is yet to be fully defined; however, it is often described as a blending of the different historical "streams" in the church. There are many unique expressions of the church, yet they are generally easy to identify within broad categories. While each generalized church category or *stream* has a multitude of emphases, styles of worship and doctrinal positions, for our purposes here, we identify three primary streams:

- **The Evangelical Stream:** emphasizing salvation by faith in the atoning death of Jesus Christ through personal conversion, the authority of Scripture, theological intellectualism,

---

4. For a description of "The Convergence Movement," see the article written by Wayne Boosahda and Randy Sly for *Twenty Centuries of Christian Worship* by Robert Webber, ed. Boosahda is the presiding bishop of the Communion of Convergence Churches USA, which is a province of the Communion of Evangelical Episcopal Churches, and Sly is a provincial bishop in the International Communion of the Charismatic Episcopal Church.

evangelism, the importance of preaching as contrasted with ritual and a *reformational* view of the church. While honoring God the Father and God the Holy Spirit, the evangelical worship emphasis is upon God the Son. A defining ministry characteristic of evangelicals is *proclamational ministry of the Gospel*, emphasizing the importance of proclaiming biblical truth to the world around us.

• **The Sacramental Stream:** emphasizing the sacramental presence of God through liturgy and rites, symbolism and signs, orthodoxy, preservation of historical episcopacy and a *historical* view of the church. While honoring God the Son and God the Holy Spirit, the sacramental worship emphasis is upon God the Father. A defining ministry characteristic of sacramentalists is *incarnational ministry of the Gospel*, demonstrating spirituality through ministry to human needs and material signs and symbols.

• **The Charismatic Stream:** emphasizing the free expression of the gifts and person of the Holy Spirit, especially in expressive praise and in miraculous signs and wonders, practical theology and focus on life and ministry in the Spirit, and an informal *New Testament* view of the church. While honoring God the Father and God the Son, the charismatic worship emphasis is upon God the Holy Spirit. A defining ministry characteristic of charismatics is *supernatural ministry of the Gospel*, emphasizing miraculous personal experience with God through His Word and power.

Has God sovereignly prompted the formation of these distinct streams within the church, each of which seems to focus on a person of the Trinity, to more fully manifest His distinct but inseparable Persons in the earth? And if so, will there be an even greater manifestation of His fullness through the church as we acknowledge the distinct streams of His body while seeking to allow them to flow together in unity? Perhaps it is only in diversity that all of the distinguishing characteristics in the Godhead can be fully displayed and understood.

We see many examples of this Holy Spirit-inspired convergence of the streams of worship. A significant number of evangelicals are adopting more traditionally Pentecostal expressions, such as more lively worship and anointing the sick with oil. Multitudes of charismatics and Pentecostals worldwide are searching into sacramentalism and orthodoxy. Millions of Roman Catholics, Episcopalians and other liturgical traditionalists are now openly evangelical or charismatic. Expressions of church unity and mutual cooperation are arising at an unprecedented level. Walls of division are crumbling in spite of the best efforts of those who prefer them to remain. This phenomenon is not being planned or coordinated by anyone. Unity must be born of God. History is littered with the remains of failed human attempts to unify the church. Yet it appears that God Himself is bringing it about on a worldwide basis. It is unlikely to result in a humanly coordinated, preplanned organizational unity. What is more probable is that we will experience an organic *unity of purpose*, resulting in mutual recognition and increased cooperation. Convergence, along with other related issues, could be a sign of a new reformation of the church as God prepares us to fulfill His mandate.

In fact, earthly unity in the church is not an end in itself, but rather, a starting point for finishing the work with which we are tasked—the preaching of the Gospel and the discipling of believers among every people group, language group and nation of the world.

My own spiritual journey has led me to commit my life to the Great Commission while chiefly functioning out of an expression of convergence that is explained further in chapter 1 and in an appendix. Frankly, I struggled with the idea of putting chapter 1 in this book at all since it is primarily about personal experiences and conclusions. My hesitation in inserting my testimony is that, far too often in contemporary Christianity, the emphasis seems to focus upon individual experiences as opposed to global issues. I hope my story serves to validate, not distract from, the greater purpose of this book.

In chapter 2 we begin in earnest to get to the intent of this offering—unity with purpose. Finishing the task of fulfilling the Great Commission will require increased collaborative effort among every branch and expression of the church in the earth. We will discuss biblical, historical, contemporary and future models for unity and cooperation in subsequent chapters.

Unity with redemptive purpose is the primary point of this book. The centerpiece of all that we will discuss is the fulfillment of the prayer of Jesus in John 17:21, that we would *"be one"* so that through our unity with God and one another *"the world may know."* As we fully embrace the Great Commandment, we will fulfill the Great Commission. The result of finishing our earthly mission will be the thundering consonant of praise to the Lamb seated upon His throne; the voice of the eternally grateful redeemed of the Lord from every tribe, people, language and nation—*the sound of rushing waters.*

I deal with many admittedly controversial subjects in this book, most without giving sufficient time to individual issues. I do not intend this to be an exhaustive study of these subjects, but rather, a plea for greater awareness, understanding and dialogue. I freely admit that the views I offer are incomplete since my personal journey of discovery is still in process and that I "know in part."[5] Yet, these issues can't wait until we are perfectly informed.

We will look at some of the specific challenges we face in the church at large and in local expressions of the church. I offer models that have biblical and historic roots that may present solutions as we move forward. Particular attention is given to the issues surrounding apostolic ministry, the need for universally recognized ecumenical church councils, and models for theological and cooperative unity, such as the Chicago-Lambeth Quadrilateral and the Lausanne Covenant.

Finally, we will consider how it is possible for the church to be both ancient and new simultaneously. While we have a

---

5. 1 Corinthians 13:12.

glorious past, the best has not yet been seen but is soon to be revealed. We live in the church's finest hour as we accept the challenges before us and cooperatively labor to finish our work on earth.

It is my conviction that we are already in the midst of a new and needed reformation of the church. "To reform" does not mean "to replace." However, it does mean "to improve upon." We can surely become much more functional than we are today by aligning ourselves with God's purpose for the end-time church. We can reach the finish line and complete our mission in the earth. We will.

This book is written in pursuit of effective unity and in the hope of providing increased understanding of how our differences do not have to be barriers to unity. My goal is to offer potential solutions for practical cooperation, so that we may swiftly finish the task of world evangelization and welcome the return of our Lord and Savior Jesus Christ.

Psalm 133:1-3: **"How good and pleasant it is when brothers live together in unity! It is like precious oil poured on the head, running down on the beard, running down on Aaron's beard, down upon the collar of his robes. It is as if the dew of Hermon were falling on Mount Zion. For there the LORD bestows his blessing, even life forevermore."**

Chapter One

———∞∞∞———

Journey and Formation

G od has His people on a journey toward His final purpose. Though we cannot always see the future with pristine clarity, we can learn from what our journey has taught us to this point. Considering where we have been and how it impacts our current thinking is an important exercise as we prepare for what is ahead. My own journey has been a discovery of the purpose and breadth of the church.

A personal testimony is not simply a collection of experiences. A testimony is, for the most part, a collection of influences. The most powerful influences, beyond the obvious influence that God exercises, are the people who impact your life. Many wonderful people have been a part of my personal journey and have greatly influenced me.

You may find my personal journey and formation relevant to your own experience or interest. Since, however, the purpose of this book is definitely not my story, if you find my personal journey tedious or unnecessary to know, simply skip this chapter.

After hearing a fiery message on heaven and hell, I knew I was a sinner who needed Jesus' forgiveness. The year was 1959 and we were in a special revival meeting under a canvas tent set up next to our church sanctuary. The strong smell of the saw-dust that covered the ground and the rich sound of hymns filled the air. I raised my hand at the invitation and was quickly met by my Sunday school teacher, who led me to the altar, where I wept aloud and prayed the sinner's prayer. I was 5 years old. This was the beginning of my spiritual journey.

What an advantage it was to be raised in a genuine Christian home. My parents, my four siblings and I were in church on Sundays and Wednesdays. This upbringing in an Independent Baptist and, subsequently, Southern Baptist tra-dition, was filled with years of Sunday school and Training Union, evangelistic sermons, Bible study, Royal Ambassadors, Lottie Moon and Annie Armstrong missionary offerings, home visitation, altar calls and "*just one more stanza of 'Just As I Am.'*" My earliest memories are filled with evangelical fervor. My parents, Oliver and Nadjy Williams, were dedicated believ-ers who actively shared their faith and lived with high moral values. They loved God, each other and their five children. Other than the run-of-the-mill sibling conflicts that families experience, our home was a place of peace. Christmas was truly Christ-centered. Easter was a celebration of a risen Christ who lived in our hearts and home in Jacksonville, Florida.

However, I had a streak of rebellion and curiosity that warred against my spiritual upbringing. Soon my life began to form into separate parts. At home, I was a typical boy growing up in the suburbs in the 1950s and '60s. I was generally well-mannered and respectful of my parents. But at school, another personality began to emerge. I became somewhat of a "class clown," spending far too much time engaging others in laugh-ter and conversation. In fact, most of my grade-school years were spent in close proximity to my teachers. It is not that they liked me all that much; it's just that they usually placed my desk right next to theirs to help control my wandering mind and proclivity to engage others in conversation. These charac-teristics, while certainly not endearing to my beleaguered teachers, have actually served me well later in life.

In the neighborhood, I developed a reputation for free-spirited fun and an adventurous spirit. Unfortunately, my "free spirit" was not behaving in a Christian manner, and my actions became increasingly shameful.

Lastly, at our local church I walked a tightrope. With my peers, I behaved as I did at school or in the neighborhood. With the adults, I acted like the good Christian boy that I really wanted to be in my heart. Every time there was a revival at our church, I would make new commitments in my heart to Jesus, only to see them unravel as soon as I returned to my friends at school and the neighborhood.

My father died when I was 12. Things turned for the worse at that point. While he was being transported to the hospital in an emergency vehicle, I held my little sister Cindy in my arms and prayed that God would raise my father from the dead if necessary. Even at the funeral I still believed that he would rise. I lingered hopefully at the grave until they began throwing dirt on his casket. When he did not rise from the dead as I had planned in my 12-year-old mind, I blamed God. My conclusion: God is not real. At that very moment, it was like something inside of me shut off. For the next few years I never prayed. God became nothing to me. He was not real. I cared less and less about keeping up the fronts at church and home. My heart grew so bitter toward God that I convinced myself He did not even exist. There would be little value in sharing what happened over the next few years. The backslidden heart, living outside of a conscious acknowledgment of and submission to the Almighty, can be surprisingly evil.

It was at the age of 17, in the midst of my rebellion, when everything changed. I can't really explain why I suddenly awoke from my spiritual slumber. Perhaps it was the persistent prayers of my mother and stepfather. God's grace came, I repented of the life I had been living and, because of genuine zeal wrapped in a blanket of immaturity, I quickly became a generally obnoxious, fanatical Christian. I bought a huge Bible, wore a large cross made of nails around my neck and dedicated my life to learning everything I could about Jesus, then sharing what I learned with anyone who would listen…or just didn't escape quickly enough.

Since all I knew of the church was through my Baptist upbringing, I embarked upon a commitment to be the best Baptist I could be. My girlfriend and future wife, Sharon, simultaneously made these commitments. In fact, our mutual love for God and commitment to His call would save our marriage in the coming years. Without Sharon's depth of spirituality, flexibility and forgiveness, there would be no story to tell. Frankly, although it was difficult for us the first five years, our life together since has been the greatest single force that God has used to form me. Sharon is an anointed minister and leader in her own right. I trust her implicitly. Her counsel and encouragement have made my journey possible. Sharon is my closest confidant, constant companion and best friend.

While dating as teenagers, Sharon and I climbed a tree to talk about our relationship and our individual desire to fulfill God's purpose for our lives. Where else would teenagers go to talk? (I am, by the way, now out of my tree; a fact that many astute people would affirm.) It was there in that tree, with legs kicking the air, that Sharon turned to me and said, "God will do something worldwide with you and I am supposed to be a part of it." Little did we know at that moment the significance of those prophetic words, and the impact they would have in our lives.

As a Baptist, I was raised in a rich spiritual tradition, but one that primarily identifies itself with the first one hundred years of the church (the Apostolic Period), then skips to the canonization of the Scriptures and then picks up again somewhere from the Reformation until the present. This approach to church history left quite a few gaps, to say the least. Like most believers, I made no conscious effort to intentionally ignore the rest of the historic and contemporary church; I was simply living out my own form of Christian piety as I understood it. My personal base of ministry began in an evangelical, fundamentalist environment, and that environment had a profound impact on my formation as a minister. At age 17, I launched forward with an evangelistic zeal to convert others to Christ and with a deep commitment to found everything upon the Word of God, yet I had a very limited view of the church beyond my evangelical world. In fact, I often doubted the validity of other streams of the church altogether. I had the idea that Roman Catholics and Orthodox were not real Christians, and that all of the other Protestant churches were, at best, partially deceived. This was especially true of the chandelier-swinging, overly-emotional, holy-roller Pentecostals, who were to be avoided at all costs.

At a somewhat clandestine home prayer meeting I attended one evening, I found fellow Baptists who were studying Scripture, speaking in tongues and praying for the sick. I didn't understand it, but I definitely wanted the power and exuberant love for God that these people expressed. A 10-year-old boy in attendance that life-changing night had a profound impact on me. He stood to the side, tears rolling down his cheeks as he quietly prayed in an unknown tongue and praised God with hands raised. The innocent genuineness of this child's expression of love for Jesus began to break down the walls of resistance that surrounded my heart. Could these be the dreaded Pentecostals who had been so demonized in my mind? I found their love for God absolutely irresistible.

Later that week, I relayed this experience to our youth minister. He confessed that he, too, was a "closet charismatic" and had been reluctant to share his own experience with the Holy Spirit openly for fear of losing his job. I was emboldened to seek more after learning of his personal testimony. A well-meaning student from the nearby university found our youth group one evening not long afterward, and made desperate attempts to impel us to speak in tongues. This zealous enforcement of the charismatic experience actually set the whole process back a few months for several of us, but our desperation for more and God's faithfulness to keep us on track prevailed over our temporary disturbance.

Just a few months later, on a Baptist youth retreat, after most everyone had gone to bed, I slipped into the chapel to pour my heart out to God. That night at the altar I pleaded with God for more of Him and less of me, and after an hour of prayer, I received a glorious infilling of the Holy Spirit. I received no outward manifestation of a charismatic enablement that night, but things radically changed inwardly. I came to a new place of surrender and joy. A greater love for others was imparted to my heart that night, and a new sense of God's abiding presence and enlightenment became my daily experience in the days that followed. In time, many of the spiritual gifts generally associated with this experience were manifested in my life.

I later discovered that Epworth by the Sea, a Methodist camp located on St. Simons Island in southeastern Georgia, is the very island where John and Charles Wesley lived with their mother during their tenure in America. The church building where I prayed had originally been an Episcopal church, but was now a part of the Methodist camp. I share all of this trivia to make a point. It is no wonder that my whole spiritual journey has been one of diversity and embrace of the whole church, for even my experience with the Holy Spirit was one of ecumenical blending. For you see, I received my Pentecostal experience while at the altar of an Episcopal church on a Methodist camp while attending a Baptist youth retreat! Now that is convergence of the streams of the church!

And what became of our youth pastor? He was right after all, for he eventually lost his job over the charismatic issue. After a few more attempts to pastor churches in the Baptist tradition, he became pastor of an independent charismatic church. Ron Durham went on to become the very successful pastor of a large church in the Northeast. Sharon and I are grateful for the many ways that he helped us along the way during those formative years. At the almost certain risk of his career, he encouraged us to seek more of the Holy Spirit in our lives, conducted our marriage ceremony, helped to financially support us as missionaries, shared our love for the nations, led his congregation through a process to give their church facilities to Calvary International,[1] taught in our Bible schools, and the list goes on.

Actually, moving from a purely evangelical base to a charismatic one had a profound effect beyond the personal spiritual blessings I experienced. The baptism in the Holy Spirit greatly enhanced my journey toward recognizing the broader church. This experience not only caused me to evaluate my former spiritual traditions, it also propelled me into a world previously unknown to me—the universal body of Christ.

Early in Sharon's and my walk with God, we began to minister to the broken and needy. At first, we were ministering to those who were trapped in the drug culture of the early seventies. This soon led us to the most wounded of our society as we moved into inner-city ministry. Living and ministering in the inner-city while working closely with a Methodist pastor and a Presbyterian pastor brought us into a whole new world of cross-cultural, cross-economic, cross-racial and cross-denominational experiences.

From our two-year inner-city experience we moved into ministry at an affluent, suburban Episcopal church. This was as much a cross-cultural adventure for us as the inner city had been. We learned so much about pastoring a growing church, and building a successful organization; and it was during this time that we first learned about sacramental theology and the episcopal form of church government.

I was further catapulted along in my journey by our missionary endeavors when, at age 27, we moved with our four young children to Central America. A delightful discovery awaited us at the language school we attended in San Jose, Costa Rica. We were in classes with many sincere Christians from

---

1. Calvary International (CI) was founded in 1981 by Daniel and Sharon Williams in response to their personal missionary call. Calvary currently works in more than 40 countries around the world, and has trained tens of thousands of pastors and leaders along with planting churches and Bible schools around the world. Jerry Williamson has been the president of CI since 2000.

every sector of the church. How joyous it was to mix with believers who shared our passion for Christ and His commission, who experienced along with us the challenges of learning a language and living in a new and different culture, all the while being so distinct from one another in our doctrine and worship practices. We later discovered that it is common to encounter more visible cooperation and open fellowship among different branches of the church in many nations of the world. No doubt, the increased outside pressures of persecution and spiritual resistance often encountered in these places contribute to this visible unity.

Our first year of missionary experience was particularly valuable to our formation because we closely worked with a group of Costa Rican nationals. This not only accelerated our language acquisition, it taught me a great deal about the internationalization of the worldwide church. For one year, I was the only resident American missionary working with this particular association of approximately 120 churches.[2] I served under the energetic apostolic leadership of Edgar and Carlos Chacon and the elder statesman of the group, David Barrantes. We were in the midst of a nationwide revival that was sweeping Costa Rica and that endured with intensity for about five years and lasted for a total of approximately 10 years. There was tremendous unity among the pastors and amazing church growth among every sector of the church, particularly the Pentecostals. During those precious years, I learned to work with and under the authority of non-Americans, and to partner with many different groups, both denominational and parachurch. I met many outstanding missionaries from every branch of the church and came to understand that many of the denominations I had previously disregarded as irrelevant were actually doing great work in the nations of the world.

---

2. Las Iglesias Evangelicas Nacionales, led by its president, Edgar Chacon, was a Costa Rican-birthed and -managed organization that grew to approximately two hundred churches during the 1980s. It was loosely modeled upon the Assemblies of God church structure.

Our small but dynamic Pentecostal/charismatic network of churches was growing exponentially with the nationwide revival Costa Rica was experiencing. There were services every night, seven days a week. On Sundays, I preached as often as five times in five different locations, all the while attending language school four hours a day, five days a week. After a little over a year of working like this, the revival was growing, but I was wearing down physically, spiritually and emotionally. Our four children were suffering from their "missing-in-action father," and Sharon and I were under the strain of it all. I knew there had to be a better way for me to function personally. God made a way.

I learned many lessons, both positive and negative, while serving as a part of this apostolically led network of churches. The lack of formality and agreed-upon procedures in their structure was more than compensated by the constant contact with their apostolic leaders. Still, the lack of clearly understood lines of authority and procedures did cause many problems as the network grew. My experience from direct involvement in that apostolic church network, as well as several others with which I have worked, is that there is a maturation process through which every movement must pass. Using historically proven models can accelerate the maturation process, but if done too quickly, or without exponential character development of its leaders, administrative excellence, good communications and sound procedural systems, the final result is a movement that stalls or even fails.

In response to the growing demands for trained leaders, and to get my own life back into equilibrium, I teamed up[3] with three other missionaries and two Costa Rican ministers

---

3. The initial ministry team of Cristo Al Mundo: Jimmy Coleman (C.R.), Doug Fischer (U.S.A.), Patrick McDermott (C.R.), Jim Puhr (U.S.A.), Don Sims (U.S.A.) and Daniel Williams (U.S.A.). Don Sims originally brought together and envisioned the individual missionaries and nationals to form this new school, and Jimmy Coleman was chosen by all to be the first director. This was the first of many schools begun on this pattern through Calvary International that have been and are continuing to be planted around the world.

to found a Bible training center. Cristo Al Mundo (Christ to the World) went on to train more than four thousand leaders over the next few years in Costa Rica. I maintained my connection to Las Iglesias Evangelicas Nacionales while in Costa Rica, but within two years we, along with four other families, moved to Ecuador to open our second school. In 1986, at the urging of our ministry leadership, Sharon and I moved our family back home to build a strong foundation for what would become a worldwide ministry.

Over the 19 years I served as president of Calvary International, we always networked with many other ministries and denominations both in the United States and in the nations where we operated. Those years, serving along with the many nationals, missionaries and the staff of Calvary International, along with the many leaders of other organizations networked together for the cause of Christ, were the most formative years of my life. We sought God together, played together, prayed and fasted together, traveled the world together, and saw more fruit than any of us could have ever dreamed. I am eternally grateful to all of those who worked so hard, and are still laboring to extend God's kingdom throughout the earth.

As I came to know many wonderful believers in Christ outside of the denomination of my upbringing and initial ministry formation, questions began to arise in my mind. When my own journey led me to study the early church fathers, the steady advance of the church throughout history, and the amazing diversity of theology, piety, emphasis and expression, it was a delightful and empowering experience. I am still growing and learning. I desire to intellectually grasp, spiritually perceive and emotionally feel a connection to the historic, contemporary and future body of Christ that I could have easily missed with my previous myopic way of viewing the church, past and present.

The Hebrew style of storytelling can be difficult for those unfamiliar with its nonsequential nature. It often involves picking up the story at whatever element seems convenient for the point being made at that moment. Therefore, in this Jewish tradition of anecdotal oration, there is frequent starting and stopping, repeating of details and negligible concern for sequential delivery. So, in the Hebrew style of storytelling, I will change the sequence of my story and back up for a moment.

At age 19, I met a man who would have a significant impact over practically my entire adult life. Costa Deir would become a spiritual father to me. For 25 years, we would find ways to be together, though our paths generally kept us apart. I always deeply appreciated the postcards he sent me from the far reaches of the globe. We spent thousands of hours together, from Costa Rica to South Korea, from my home to his, from America to Taiwan. Long before I actually met his precious wife "Mama Ruth," I felt like I knew her. He spoke of her often, and also bestowed continual praise and adoration upon his children. Over time, I came to know and love them all. In the days after his death, while staying in his home, I found myself staring at his daughter and sons, Alexis, Salim, Tim and John. They each, along with their spouses and children, reflect a wonderful blend of Costa and Mama Ruth in their countenance and character. Costa went to heaven first, then Mama Ruth. I still feel the sting of their departure from this life. I called him Dad.

Dad gave me more treasures than I could ever recount. Costa called me "son" from the start; and, like a father, he used most of our time together to constantly teach me leadership principles that he had learned over a lifetime. Those principles, always meticulously verified in accompanying Scriptures, helped to form me and propel me along in my journey. He helped me to love and appreciate the peoples of the world, especially the African[4] people, long before I personally experienced them for myself. He passed along to me deep appreciation and love for the unknown national pastors in obscure places around the globe. But, perhaps the most important values he modeled

---

4. In his role with Elim Fellowship and its worldwide network of pastors and missionaries, Costa Deir oversaw more than four thousand churches in East Africa for many years.

for me were his intense love for God, his passion for his family and, especially, his love for the whole church—the church without borders and without walls. He would go and train leaders anywhere in the world, no matter how remote and with any branch of the church that would have him. And have him they did. He gave his whole life to training leaders.

I began to understand just how broad his impact was when we were together for two weeks at the Global Consultation on World Evangelization in Seoul, South Korea. Thousands of mission leaders from around the world were there. The vast majority of those present were from Third World nations. As we walked together from session to session, or to breakfast, lunch or dinner, it was always the same routine. We were stopped every few feet by one or several pastors and leaders greeting and thanking Costa for the impact he had had on their lives, churches or nations. This happened about a hundred times every day for two weeks. It wasn't just the quantity of people that constantly surrounded Dad, or even the stories they told me that so impressed me; it was the broad variety of people from every segment of the world and every branch of the church. There were internationally known evangelists, pastors of huge churches, denominational leaders, and pastors and leaders from obscure, little-known parts of the globe. There were such a variety of shapes and colors and sizes. There were so many divergent languages and cultures and theological positions represented in those who pressed around him. Many turned to me to say things like, "He saved my life," "He saved my marriage" or "He has helped our leaders more than we can say." I was proud of being with him and humbled by his stature.

Dad loved the whole church, and they loved him for it. Though most of his life he worked within the ministry of Elim, based in Lima, N.Y., he always gave himself to the whole body of Christ. Faithful to his beloved Elim to the end, he never ceased doing whatever he could to bless as many as possible, without regard to what branch of the church they belonged. Costa had a uniqueness about him that is world-renowned.

His generous spirit deeply impacted my life. I am but one of his many spiritual sons around the globe. I hope to emulate something of what he gave me.

About the time I met Costa, another man began to reach out to me. He would also become a notable person in my development as a man of God. Russell Linenkohl and his wife, Barbara, helped Sharon and me through the troubles we experienced in our first few years of marriage. Russell was always there for me in the major decision moments of my life, and would ultimately become a key player and co-laborer in the development of Calvary International. But Russell's "fathering" was somewhat different than Costa's.

Russell is what I would call "a gentleman's gentleman." Much of his early mentoring of me focused on practical things. Whereas Costa taught me principles, Russell taught me practices. Through his influence, I began to develop a greater sensitivity to the feelings and needs of others. Like many ministers, I had a greater kindness and compassion for the broken and needy than for the person working at my side. Russell helped change that. He taught me social graces, encouraged me to learn all I could about how to manage an organization with excellence and gave an unfailing example of love for his beloved Barbara.

Russell, too, seemed to see the church as being "without walls" and without limits. He helped me learn to appreciate and genuinely express care for the work of others. Though very much a charismatic in his spirituality, he encouraged me to network with as many believers as possible. He gave me an example of enthusiastic relationship-building, of servanthood ministry and of an unfaltering love for his heavenly Father. Though he is one of my fathers in the Lord, he served faithfully under my leadership and even permitted me a role as his pastor. I am eternally indebted to him and Barbara.

I am giving such detail about these two men, because each took a role as an apostolic father who cared for my soul while provoking me to greater levels of spirituality, accountability and effective ministry. There is a tremendous need for this kind of apostolic shepherding throughout the church. Their influence, along with that of a few others,[5] has helped to form my view of what true leadership should look like—more like that of a father than that of an executive.

Over time, and with the helpful influence of so many, I came to appreciate the whole church in all of its rich diversity, especially the primary streams that have historically manifested themselves. These streams have been identified by many as the liturgical/sacramental stream, the evangelical/fundamental stream and the charismatic/Pentecostal stream. From my roots in evangelicalism in the Baptist tradition, entry into the charismatic/Pentecostal world was a significant leap. Yet my entry into the liturgical/sacramental world was at least as profound. As I experienced evangelicalism, Pentecostalism and, still later, sacramentalism, I developed a peculiar blend of preferences in worship and doctrine. For the sake of unity and cooperation with others, and for the expediency of the work in which I was involved, I have at appropriate times laid aside my preferences. Now my life is a daily learning experience of discovery and blending of these streams. I have found that sacramentalism and orthodoxy provide a sound framework within which evangelical mission and charismatic expression can function.

We each carry certain values forward from the stream from which we come. Yet when it comes to building unity in the church, we must often downplay our own preferences for the sake of cooperation. If we allow one another differences of emphasis, yet work hard to find points of agreement, then we have the basis of true unity and cooperation in the body of Christ. Respecting differences and believing that God is the author of these differences is central to our mutual success.

As a result of these personal experiences and tendencies, I have never been comfortable identifying with only one stream

---

5. The apostle Paul referenced having "fathers" of a spiritual nature. I, too, have been blessed by spiritual parents such as the aforementioned Costa & Ruth Deir and Russell & Barbara Linenkohl and, additionally, Paul & Dee Goodwin.

of the church. I have looked for ways to functionally embrace the various branches.

For a number of years, I searched for others who shared my enthusiasm for studying the historical church and blending the diversity of the various streams into a contemporary expression. This search led me to the Communion of Evangelical Episcopal Churches (CEEC) in early 1997. My conversations with Van Gayton, the pastor of a large Assembly of God church in Buffalo, N.Y., who was ordained a priest in the CEEC and later consecrated a bishop, led me into a communication process with the CEEC House of Bishops. After a few months of discussion, they offered me the opportunity to join them; and, considering my background in church planting and worldwide ministry, they offered to receive me into their communion as a bishop.

The Communion of Evangelical Episcopal Churches is an extraordinary gathering of brethren who are truly committed to God's will. I found them to be refreshingly open to the Lord and His whole body. I had no reservations about joining their communion from a fraternal point of view. I value their fellowship to this day and continue to personally grow through our relationship. However, I hesitated to join them in full communion as one of their clergy because I perceived a resolve in the CEEC, during that period of its development as a communion, to express their faith with high-church Anglicanism with a Celtic accentuation as their center of emphasis.[6]

In the first place, I did not at that time fully appreciate the rich vibrancy and value of the Celtic Church as a potential contemporary model. Further study has matured my view. Actually, as modern culture has evolved, a new form of pagan

---

6. The Communion of Evangelical Episcopal Churches, as with any emerging organization, continued to develop and grow in its views and practices. While still maintaining a high regard for Celtic Christianity and traditional Anglicanism, the CEEC reasserted its conviction to emphasize the "essentials" of the faith as put forth in the primary historical creeds, and to foster and embrace a diversity of practices in its clergy, members and churches.

tribalism has developed, especially among those of Western culture. Rather than small, isolated tribes in obscure villages, we now have what I would classify as "affinity tribalism." Affinity tribalism is based on social, political, religious or economic similarities rather than the traditional factors of location, culture, language or race. Urban centers, especially those of the world's largest cities, are filled with affinity tribes. Dr. Donald McGavran's[7] breakthrough studies on "people groups" have significantly contributed to the understanding of how masses of people can become so isolated from other groups that may be in close proximity that they remain practically unreached or untouched by others. This isolation of specific people groups in the midst of masses presents new challenges for the church today. These distinctive groupings of people are growing in number and often demonstrate an increased antagonism toward others. St. Patrick's success in winning the Celtic pagan tribes of his day with innovative approaches to ministry provides potential insight for finishing the task of world evangelization today, especially in post-Christian Western nations.

Second, as I considered joining the CEEC at that time, a high-church expression of Anglicanism was an issue for me. Anglicanism has a theological richness and historical structure that I highly esteem. The challenge for me was what I observed to be the CEEC's well-thought-out and intentional pursuit of worship as practiced in high-church Anglican culture. The Anglican Church culture is a mix of ceremony and practices that date back hundreds of years, or in some cases, nearly two thousand years. It is beautiful and awe-inspiring. It is rich with symbolism and form. It captures the texture of historic Roman Catholic and Orthodox worship, with a clearly reformational bent. I deeply value the Anglican Church, and seriously considered becoming an Episcopal priest as early as 1978, but have

---

7. Donald McGavran was born in India to missionary parents and became a third-generation missionary himself in 1923. He is considered to be one of the foremost missiologists of the past century. His breakthrough book, *Bridges of God,* has become a standard for modern missionary strategists.

not regarded the Episcopal priesthood as the best center from which I can operate and fulfill God's destiny and purpose for my life. Though offered the opportunity, I chose in 1981 not to seek the priesthood in the Episcopal Church U.S.A. I made this decision prayerfully and thoughtfully after serving on the ministry staff of St. Peter's Episcopal Church[8] as a "visiting clergy" for three and a half years. I spent many hours in dialogue with Bishop Frank Cerveny, the bishop of Florida at that time, and with Father John Bell, the rector of the church I served. It became clear to me that I was not a perfect fit within that denomination. This was a very hard decision for me because of the profound respect that I had for both Bishop Cerveny and Father Bell. Bishop Cerveny was the very first bishop with whom I had any personal contact, and to this day I appreciate and emulate the model of a bishop that he faithfully demonstrated. When I first went to work in his diocese, he told me that I brought a "gift" to them. He stated to me at that time that he appreciated my evangelical/charismatic bent and felt that I would offer something positive to the diocese. Actually, it was I who received more gifts than I could possibly recount through my association with Bishop Cerveny, Father Bell, and all of the wonderful staff and members of St. Peter's.

While I love the episcopal system of church government and the liturgical/sacramental approach to worship, I do not so strongly embrace much of the symbolism that comes with traditional high-church Anglicanism, especially as often practiced in the United States by the Protestant Episcopal Church. It is not a matter of its validity or value, but simply that God has called me to chiefly function out of an expression of convergence that is more centristic and reflective of all of the primary streams without a preference for one. Many evangelicals and Pentecostals around the world are moving back to a historical expression of Anglicanism or Orthodoxy. I understand, appreciate and applaud this phenomenon. However, there are those

---

8. St. Peter's Episcopal Church is located in Jacksonville, Florida.

like myself who are called to a center in the convergence of the primary historical streams of evangelicalism, Pentecostalism and sacramentalism in a contemporary expression. We are searching for the right balance and application of the different streams in our daily life and ministry. We look at historical Anglicanism, Eastern Orthodoxy and Roman Catholicism and see much to value, but are concerned with the likely potential of adopting inappropriate practices for our current ministries that are rooted in a church culture that is hundreds, if not thousands, of years old, and while appropriate for the past, may not be suitable for today or the future.

In his book *A Church to Believe In*, Peter Moore used an example from D. Robert Webber's classic book *Evangelicals on the Canterbury Trail* to speak to the issue of using caution as we embrace aspects of the church that may be new to us as individuals: "Many who have come late to these things in their Christian journey will appreciate the zeal with which these converts share their discoveries. However, one of these modern Canterbury pilgrims whom [Dr. Robert] Webber interviewed[9] caught my attention by likening himself to a boa constrictor, which swallows its prey whole and then proceeds to digest it. He seized upon Anglicanism 'from an impulse of the heart' and swallowed it whole, without chewing. He was still digesting what he had swallowed. I read this story with interest, possibly because my own experience was so different from his. And the Anglicanism that this zestful convert had swallowed was not the sort that appeals to me… His, I think, was a conversion to mystery, authority, and tradition, in reaction to an evangelical upbringing that was seriously wanting in these areas of church life. But a reactionary attitude can blind us to the good in what we are leaving behind or the possible evils in what we embrace."[10]

I should say here that Dr. Webber has had a pivotal impact on my own understanding and growth. He is perhaps the most

---

9. From an excerpt of Webber's *Evangelicals on the Canterbury Trail*.
10. Peter C. Moore, *A Church to Believe In*, Latimer Press, Bainbridge, Ohio, 1994, p. 178.

articulate and learned expositor on the subject of "convergence." While my own reaction is more like Dr. Moore's, I have the deepest respect and appreciation for Dr. Webber's personal journey and the lessons he has learned from it.

There is a common tendency in every segment of the church to "swallow whole and digest later." When those raised in traditional churches become born again, they often reject everything from their church background, declare all the past to be "dead religion" and swallow evangelicalism whole without much caution or discernment. Evangelicals who receive the baptism in the Holy Spirit often do the same with their past tradition and run toward their new experience with complete abandon. Every new experience or exotic doctrine is immediately seized upon. I also see this tendency in those discovering the riches of historical sacramentalism. They often become enamored with the symbolism and the giddy joy of discovering that they have a historical past. In fact, in this case the past may become an unhealthy obsession. In each case, this "swallow whole and digest later" approach seems unwise at best and possibly perilous.

There are those who may never "swallow whole" the entire Anglo-Catholic or Orthodox traditions, but who embrace many of their principal elements, such as the episcopal system of government, continuing apostolic ministry, the importance of relevant historical traditions and symbolism, the value of ceremony, recognition and practice of the sacraments and sacramentalism, the historical creeds and doctrinal orthodoxy. They desire to blend strengths of the different streams into a contemporary version of the historical church. This contemporary version should carry forth the unbroken stream of continuity of apostolic tradition and succession from the founding of the church, but also incorporate the different truths revealed within the primary historical streams in a current expression that is as relevant to the end times as it is to the ancient times.

Though I continue to grow in my understanding and appreciation of historic Christianity as expressed in Anglicanism, my own calling has led me toward a more centrist position within the convergence of evangelicalism, Pentecostalism and sacramentalism.

I have a deep admiration for the episcopal system of church government, with its emphasis on apostolic order. Years of experience in church planting and translocal ministry have taught me the value of accountability, oversight, synergism and encouragement that comes from being a functional part of a leadership team. My Baptist upbringing, along with many years of involvement in the charismatic stream, encourages independence and autonomy. This attitude of self-reliance goes against what I see in Scripture and has been repeatedly discredited in my own ministry experiences.

While working around the world, I have had the opportunity to observe and directly participate in many church movements. With rare exception, the most successful church movements utilize some system of apostolic oversight and organization. While using many different titles and terms, these movements adopt long-standing practices of accountability and structure to preserve their fruit and to multiply their efforts. We will discuss this in more detail in another chapter.

These are a few of the highlights that have played a significant role in my formation and journey. I have omitted many of the important events and influences that may have some importance or interest to some who read this, so I have included an appendix of additional information if you are so interested.

At this writing, my heart is filled with excitement and anticipation of the near future. I truly believe that God is bringing about a new day for His church. Now is the time to seek Him with all of our hearts and search out all of His ways that we might more fully reflect His glory in the earth and finish the task with which He has entrusted us.

The journey continues.

Key Discussion Points:

1. The personal journey of the author.
2. The value of spiritual influences through people and circumstances along the way.
3. The importance of finding your center and place.

Questions:

1. What spiritual influences have impacted your life and significantly helped to form you?
2. Who are the three primary people who have helped shape you, and what is it about their faith that caused you to accept their influence?

Chapter Two

—⊶∞⊶—

Unity with Purpose

Since heaven will provide complete and lasting unity in the church, is unity on earth important? Why not just nudge along in our own stream of faith and give no real concern or effort to Christian unity and cooperation? Can't we comfortably cherish and nourish our own traditions, preferred styles of worship and doctrinal emphases and avoid conflict by simply disassociating ourselves from others who are different than us? The answers to these questions are simple: Unity is not an option. Jesus desires and commands it, and unity is an essential key to finishing the task that Jesus commissioned.

Let us further explore these answers:

• **Jesus desires and commands it.** For two thousand years, the prayer of Jesus has been at work in the heavenlies: *"that all of them may be one... as we are one."*[1] Our "oneness" as the body of Christ, therefore, is God's will and must become our priority. Whether we desire it, work

---

1. John 17:21-22.

toward it or even believe in unity, ultimately we cannot prevent the will and power of God from bringing it forth. Jesus said: *"'Love the* LORD *your God with all your heart and with all your soul and with all your strength and with all your mind;' and, 'Love your neighbor as yourself.'"*[2] This directive from Christ Himself, often referred to as the "Great Commandment,"[3] is an explicit charge to the church to visibly walk in love toward God and man. Both vertical and horizontal love is required for our love to be pleasing to God. These are not suggestions, but commands. Jesus' prayer for unity will ultimately prevail because He wills it and commands it.

- **Unity is an essential key to finishing the task that Jesus commissioned.** Since *"'this gospel of the kingdom will be preached in the whole world'"*[4] and will produce the *"great multitude"* from *"every nation, tribe, people and language,"* then we must remove every hindering obstacle to cooperatively finish the task. We are to be one so that we may present to the world around us a proper representation of God. A significant part of our witness to the peoples of the earth is set forth by Jesus: *"'A new commandment I give you: Love one another. As I have loved you, so you must love one another.* **All men will know that you are my disciples if you love one another.'"**[5] Visible unity reveals God's love. Our historic disunity has frequently had a significant negative effect upon the demonstration of the power of the Gospel to change the hearts of mankind. Unbelievers often point to our disunity as a reason to reject our message.

---

2. Luke 10:2.
3. While the passage in Luke 10:2 does not separate love for God and love for your neighbor as two distinct commandments, in Matthew 22:37-40, the "Great Commandment" is separated into two separate commandments, with the first described as "greatest" and the second as "like it."
4. Matthew 24:14.
5. John 13:34-35.

But not only should unity be a powerful demonstration of our message, it is vital for finishing our work on the earth. To fulfill the Great Commission will require collaborative effort beyond what has ever existed. Unfortunately, duplication and mixed messages have often delayed the work of God. Even if cross-denominational strategic partnerships are beyond our current reach, increased communication among churches and ministries would improve the situation. Respectfully informing others of plans for ministry in a particular area or among a specific group could mean less duplication and greater productivity for all. At the very least, attempts to communicate with one another may reduce friction that results from the lack of mutual acknowledgment. After all, the spiritual and material needs around us are so many. Other Christians who may be targeting or working among the group that we are attempting to reach may be the answer to our own prayer to the "Lord of the harvest" to "send forth laborers." In simple terms, the harvest is so great and God's desire for all to be saved is so clear that we must lay aside every temptation to isolate and insulate ourselves from others.

Many years ago, I attended a missions conference sponsored by Life Christian Church[6] in St. Louis, Missouri. There, displayed on a banner suspended high above a huge stage, were words that pierce and motivate my heart to this very day: **"TO THE ENDS OF THE EARTH FOR HIS PLEASURE."** It is now the hour to change our behavior toward one another in the body of Christ for the sake of pleasing our glorious Savior and of the Gospel going forward to the ends of the earth.

Since God Himself is the creator of diversity, it is reasonable to accept and value the differences and unique expressions within the body of Christ, the church of the Firstborn. But while much good comes from our diversity, is division necessary? Can we be distinct without divorcing ourselves from one another? We have become so accustomed to division

---

6. Life Christian Church, pastored by Rick Shelton.

and brokenness in the body of Christ that it now seems normal and unchangeable. But is division the norm that God wants for His people? Is our disunity and brokenness really unchangeable, or is it possible that the true problem is that we have lost our confidence in the efficacy of Jesus' prayer? Most Christians do not believe that God is pleased with the rancor, judgmentalism and outright rejection of validity that so often characterizes the different branches of the church. Lesslie Newbigin, in commenting on the apostle Paul's perspective of factions in the church, writes: "We may further test the strength of Paul's language by examining what he says about the factions in the Church at Corinth. When he hears that the Corinthians are beginning to call themselves by the names of rival party leaders, including his own, he expresses his horror and astonishment in a series of very violent phrases: 'Is Christ divided? Was Paul crucified for you? Or were you baptized into the name of Paul?' These rhetorical questions show how any breach in the unity of the Church was in violent contradiction to the very heart of the Gospel as Paul understood it."[7] It is time for the church today to become as vehement against division as was the apostle Paul in his day.

I recently heard a fellow pastor use the same kind of "very violent phrases" to which Newbigin referred. As we downed our salads at a local café, my friend Tim Lusk[8] and I discussed the process of unity in our city and throughout the church worldwide. Tim's comments grew increasingly profound and I scrambled for a napkin and pen as he thoughtfully declared: "If we are truly Trinitarian, then we believe that God has revealed Himself to mankind as unity in diversity as Father, Son and Holy Spirit. Lack of unity in the church is a repudiation of the very nature of God.

---

7. Lesslie Newbigin, *The Household of God*, Paternoster Press, London. First published 1953 (SCM Press Ltd.), reprinted 1998, p. 86.
8. Tim Lusk is co-pastor of Christian Family Chapel in Jacksonville, Florida and is a fellow board member of Mission First Coast, a movement to foster unity through prayer and cooperation so that the northeast region of Florida may be transformed for Christ.

Division gives a false image of God to the world and borders on blasphemy." The power of his statements captivated my thoughts and struck a chord deep in my soul. The strongholds of division will be overcome only when we come to abhor them, disown them and aggressively *"press on to take hold"*[9] of the unity brought about by what Christ did on the cross. The process that removed the enmity between God and man is the same process that destroys division between us on the earth—the cross. *"For he himself is our peace, who has made the two one and has destroyed the barrier, the dividing wall of hostility."*[10] Unity has already been accomplished for us by Jesus' sacrifice. What remains is for us to believe it and take hold of it by laying hold of the cross. This is not accomplished by human effort to "get along," but by acknowledging what Christ attained for us *"through the cross, by which he put to death* [our] *hostility."*[11]

As we endeavor to address divisions in the church world-wide, we face many obstacles. Overcoming the many points of diversity of doctrine and custom is difficult enough, but with a two thousand year history of entrenched divisions, our past makes true unity today all the more difficult. How hard will it be to overcome our legacy of bad behavior toward one another, not to mention those outside of the church? Only with God's grace and our intent will things change radically, but change they will. Thankfully, our past is not the only road map for our future.

In May 1995, I had a brief taste of what is to come. We were in Seoul, South Korea, praying hand in hand. To my left was a top leader of the Assemblies of God of Brazil. To my right was a leading executive of the Southern Baptist Convention from the United States. In fact, our prayer circle of 10 consisted of leaders from different denominations, divergent streams of the church, various mission organizations, and races and cultures from around the world. In the huge auditorium where we gathered, hundreds more circles like ours joined in passionate petition as

9. Philippians 3:12.
10. Ephesians 2:14.
11. Ephesians 2:16.

over ten thousand leaders prayed for the completion of the Great Commission. We prayed "Korean style," which means everyone prayed out loud at once. It was very, very loud. Deafening, in fact. Thunderous. Like the sound of rushing waters.

For two weeks we gathered at the Global Consultation on World Evangelization (GCOWE)[12] to pray, hear from internationally recognized Christian leaders from across the globe, build relationships, share information and form strategic partnerships. This was neither the first nor last event of this type.

That moment of prayer encircled by such diversity was for me a dream come true. My heart has yearned for unity in Christ's body. Organizational unity seems impossible, but organic unity is absolutely necessary. To finish the work Christ gave us will require unprecedented cooperation. Much of the world has received the Gospel, yet the most difficult-to-reach for reasons of resistance, hostile governments, geography, culture or religion are yet ahead. We need innovative strategies and specialized methods to penetrate walls of resistance to the Gospel in these areas.

Perhaps our past divisions, which led to so much diversity, actually helped the church develop specializations that will meet unique needs. Where, for instance, would world evangelization be without the many parachurch organizations that have specialized and developed so many wonderful strategies and tools? Entire denominations, movements and educational institutions have emerged with different approaches and productive ministries. Much good has come from our diversity.

On the other hand, think of the opportunities lost and the resources wasted for lack of unity and cooperation in the universal church. Can we win this battle against the kingdom of darkness while divided against one another? The most difficult-to-reach regions of the world still await the Gospel of

---

12. The purpose of GCOWE '95 was to build momentum toward the fulfillment of the goal of a church for every people and the Gospel for every people by the year 2000. Leaders from around the world gathered for nine days in Seoul, South Korea, as a part of the AD 2000 & Beyond Movement.

Jesus Christ. The people in these nations are often trapped behind hostile and historically entrenched walls of false religions and governments who want no foreign intrusion. With these difficult circumstances in place, can any segment of the church afford to remain independent of all others and stubbornly plow ahead alone? Can we finish the task without unprecedented strategic cooperation? Even with the best-laid strategic plans and unlimited resources, our efforts are doomed to fail without God's anointing and blessing. And we can experience the full impact of God's blessing and anointing only when we come together in Holy Spirit-initiated unity.[13]

To the average Christian in America, the walls of separation between denominations and streams of the church are more blurred than ever. People choose local churches for many reasons today, giving far less regard to specific styles of worship, church structure or doctrine. Though this trend of ignoring fundamental differences may seem sinister to the clergy, theologians or traditionalists, God may well be using it to bring us together on a grassroots level. Bible studies, prayer groups and parachurch ministry involvements of every type by laypeople, as well as constant exposure to sincere Christians of every stream in the workplace, on the soccer fields and in other daily life connections, contribute to a sense of spiritual similarity among laypeople. Meanwhile, the clergy, theologians and traditionalists tend to keep to their own streams and slug it out as always. In this case, it seems that the laity are ahead of the clerical leaders as we are led by God toward visible solidarity.

The proliferation of contemporary Christian music, especially of worship songs, has increased the pace of the advance toward unity. Not surprisingly, God has touched the hearts of His people, regardless of their denominational affiliation, with a desire for deeper, more meaningful personal and public worship. Interestingly, as individuals and congregations have drawn closer to God in meaningful worship, they have moved closer to one

---

13. Psalm 133:1-3.

another in motivation, experience and style. An often-used illustration in marriage counseling is that of an equilateral triangle. Picture God at the top of the triangle and the spouses at the two bottom corners. As each spouse moves closer to God, they automatically draw closer to one another. Worship seems to have the same effect, even while we are wholly unaware of it. For the most part, without human intentionality, contemporary worship music has done more for Christian unity worldwide than anyone on earth could have planned. God is at work.

Christian media continue to exert a profound global influence on Christian unity. From local Christian radio to national and international broadcasts, from publishing houses to the Internet, God continues to use the media, not only as a tool of evangelism but as a unifier of thought and experience. On a typical Sunday morning, I may turn on the television and check in on the services and sermons from 3 to 10 different churches from across the nation before I attend my own. While driving across town on any day or night, I may have this same experience by radio. When else in history has this been possible? What effect is this cross-pollination of theology and styles having upon us all? Again, God is at work.

In practically every direction, I see more and more examples of God preparing His church for the final thrust of the Gospel to every tribe, people, language and nation. Organic unity will be a major factor as we make Jesus' last commandment our first priority.

Ultimately, there *will* be unity. Jeremiah 32:38-39 prophetically declares: *"'They will be my people, and I will be their God. I will give them singleness of heart and action, so that they will always fear me for their own good and the good of their children after them.'"* Singleness of heart will come only as we have singleness of action. Singleness of action will come only as we focus our hearts on the finish line. Nothing unifies the church like the Great Commission. We will never unify around our needs; we can unite only around the needs of others. The only hope for preserving unity and guaranteeing success is to focus our hearts and actions on fulfillment of Christ's command. Perfect unity is not the goal; rather, it is the outcome of finishing the task together. It will be achieved as we cooperatively obey the Great Commission. This Gospel of the kingdom *will* be preached in all the world. Our Lord Jesus *will* come again. We *will* all hear the "sound of rushing waters" as the streams of the church flow together in praise to the Lamb. Already I hear a growing rumble. The first time I visited Niagara Falls was an illuminating experience. I expected the beauty, the majesty and energy of the falls. I expected the huge roar of the water. I did not expect the rumble to be so powerful that I could feel it in my bones as well as hear it with my ears. And now, as I survey the majesty and breadth of the church of Jesus Christ poised for the final harvest, something deep inside of my inmost being is resonating. The gates of hell are being shaken. The walls of division in the church are cracking and crumbling. God is renewing and reforming His church.

Key Discussion Points:

1. Jesus desires and commands unity.
2. Unity is an essential key to finishing the task that Jesus commissioned.
3. God is the author of diversity.
4. The convergence of the three primary streams of the church and how each emphasizes a Person of the Trinity.

Questions:

1. What are the differences between diversity and divisions?
2. Should we work to eliminate our distinctions?
3. Does the prophecy of Jeremiah 32:38-39 connect to the contemporary church?
4. As the author describes it, what is the "sound of rushing waters"?
5. Can you think of additional examples of unplanned but burgeoning unity in the church that could accelerate the fulfillment of the Great Commission?

Chapter Three

———∞∞∞———

The People of God

The ultimate purpose of God with regard to mankind is clearly understood as we contemplate Revelation 21:3: *"And I heard a loud voice from the throne saying, 'Now the dwelling of God is with men, and he will live with them. They will be his people, and God himself will be with them and be their God.'"* We find in this passage an absolute reversal of the effects of Adam's fall, and a restoration of God's intent for humankind. The Almighty is intent upon being "with" His people whom He created for His purpose and pleasure. Christ established a "superior" covenant founded on "better promises."[1] No longer can the sin and brokenness within God's people hold His desire at bay. The result of the death, burial, resurrection and ascension of Christ is an uninhibited inclusion of all who are "children of the promise"[2] into the "family of God."[3]

---

1. Hebrews 8:6.
2. Romans 9:8.
3. 1 Peter 4:17.

In 1 Peter 2:9-10 we read: *"But you are a chosen people, a royal priesthood, a holy nation, a people belonging to God, that you may declare the praises of him who called you out of darkness into his wonderful light. Once you were not a people, but now you are the people of God; once you had not received mercy, but now you have received mercy."* All who have placed their trust in Christ alone for their standing with God are grafted into the promises made to Abraham and his descendants. As we each come to Christ as individuals, we are immediately grafted into God's family, the people of God, His chosen, holy and royal priesthood.

These truths are not fanciful human inventions or vain imaginations. These are mysteries that God Himself has designed, performed and now revealed in Scripture: *"And he made known to us the mystery of his will according to his good pleasure, which he purposed in Christ, to be put into effect when the times will have reached their fulfillment—***to bring all things in heaven and on earth together under one head, even Christ. In him we were also chosen, having been predestined according to the plan** *of him who works out everything in conformity with the purpose of his will."*[4]

The church of Jesus Christ is a fulfillment of promises made long ago. It does not eliminate or supersede the promises God made to Israel; rather, it completes them. *"For I tell you that Christ has become a servant of the Jews on behalf of God's truth, to confirm the promises made to the patriarchs so that the Gentiles may glorify God for his mercy, as it is written: 'Therefore I will praise you among the Gentiles; I will sing hymns to your name.' Again, it says, 'Rejoice, O Gentiles, with his people.' And again, 'Praise the* LORD, *all you Gentiles, and sing praises to him, all you peoples.'"*[5]

So God is working out His plan and putting it into effect in the right sequence and at the proper time. King David recognized

4. Ephesians 1:9-11.
5. Romans 15:8-11.

that God maneuvers the affairs of this world according to His purpose and power when he declared, *"But the plans of the LORD stand firm forever, the purposes of his heart through all generations."*[6] Though His plans may be a mystery at times, we can know that *"surely the Sovereign LORD does nothing without revealing his plan to his servants the prophets,"*[7] and that *"he made known to us the mystery of his will according to his good pleasure."*[8]

God's eternal plan is to have sons and daughters who are in a *perfect union* with Him through a *perfect covenant*. This was intended from the beginning to be exclusively accomplished in and through Jesus.

The early church fathers often mistakenly disconnected the church from Israel. The perceived disconnection of the church from Israel did not occur immediately, but rather, developed over a long period of time. The intense rejection of Christ (and Christians) by the Jewish religious authorities created a growing wall of separation from the start. The subsequent persecution of the Jews by the Romans convinced many early believers that the Jews rightfully suffered all of the curses of the Torah found in Deuteronomy chapters 28-33, and were therefore cut off from any future blessing. Over time, the doctrine of "supersessionism"[9] and, later, the more extreme version of "replacement theology" emerged. While the word *supersession* does mean "to replace," traditionally, supersessionism does not theorize a complete replacement of Israel by the church. Rather, it holds that Israel has been *superseded* by the church in the sense that the church has been entrusted

---

6. Psalm 33:11.
7. Amos 3:7.
8. Ephesians 1:9.
9. Over the last century, the Roman Catholic Church has issued a variety of theological position papers that seem to refute the concept of replacement theology altogether, affirming that the Torah is a valid path for Jews to be saved and that the modern Jews are a direct, unbroken continuation of the biblical people of Israel, the people of God. This unofficial view is not universally accepted, and in some cases, openly rejected by church officials.

with the fulfillment of the promises of which Jewish Israel is the trustee. In this broadly held and multifarious view, the supersession of Israel by the church can represent everything from the continuation of Jewish Israel in a shared role with the church, with both having active covenants, to the more extreme view of absolute replacement of Israel by the church and annulment of all standing covenants with the Jews. This latter, extreme version of supersessionism is described as "replacement theology." In replacement theology, the concept is that the church has *replaced* Israel as the people of God since the Jews rejected Jesus (Yeshua), their promised Messiah. While some degree of supersessionism is adhered to in most segments of the church, replacement theology has been openly refuted in much of the Protestant church, but is held firmly by some evangelical and fundamentalist groups.

Another primary theological position concerning the church and its relationship to Israel is that of "dispensationalism." This system of theology concludes that God works with and relates to mankind in different ways during different time periods. In this view, there is no direct connection between Israel and the church since God dispensed His grace and covenants separately; first to Israel, then to the church. One dispensation does not necessarily replace the other. A common outcome of this position is not an *open rejection* of Israel (and therefore, modern Jews) as the people of God, but rather, a *general ambivalence* toward Israel. Not surprisingly, as with all theological positions, there exist significant variations of dispensationalism. Some modern dispensationalists see more continuity between Israel and the church, and stress that both Israel and the church compose the "people of God" and both are related to the blessings of the New Covenant.

The full nature of the church cannot be understood from the New Testament forward without a comprehension of the promises, covenants and history of the Old Testament. Dr. Andrew Hill writes: "The study of the New Testament alone leads to an inadequate picture of God's self-disclosure and His purpose for creation. The two covenants, old and new, are one divine record of God's progressive and redemptive revelation to humankind. The promise of the older covenant finds its fulfillment in the better covenant (Hebrews 12:21-24). Emphasis on one covenant over the other produces an imbalance, robbing the Word of God of its full force and distorting its one message of salvation accomplished by God within the confines of human history."[10]

Christian history, and therefore the history of the church, is inextricably linked to the unchanging plan of God that runs directly through and is eternally connected to the history of Israel. God elected Israel to be a chosen priesthood and nation to usher in the promises and covenants. Lest we forget the unique place of the Jewish people in the sacred strategy of God, we should revisit the words of the apostle Paul: *"Theirs is the adoption as sons; theirs the divine glory, the covenants, the receiving of the law, the temple worship and the promises. Theirs are the patriarchs, and from them is traced the human ancestry of Christ, who is God over all, forever praised! Amen."*[11] In further explanation of our connection to Israel, Paul stated: *"In reading this, then, you will be able to understand my insight into the mystery of Christ, which was not made known to men in other generations as it has now been revealed by the Spirit to God's holy apostles and prophets. This mystery is that through the gospel the Gentiles are heirs together with Israel, members together of one body, and sharers together in the promise in Christ Jesus."*[12] And again, *"As far as the gospel is concerned, they are enemies on your account; but as far as election is concerned, they are loved on account of the patriarchs, for God's gifts and his call are irrevocable."*[13]

It was through His chosen people, the nation of Israel, that God brought forth the Messiah and, ultimately, the church. The

---

10. Andrew E. Hill, *Enter His Courts with Praise*, Grand Rapids, Baker Books, 1993, p. xxii (Introduction).
11. Romans 9:4-5.
12. Ephesians 3:4-6.
13. Romans 11:28-29.

connection of the church to Israel and Israel to the church has been misunderstood, denied, resented and attacked, but it cannot be eliminated. When we get to the heavenly city, New Jerusalem, the historic capital of the Jews, inscribed on the 12 gates will be the names of the 12 tribes of Israel.[14] The 12 foundations of the walls will be inscribed with the names of 12 more Jews—the 12 apostles of the Lamb.[15] And when we behold the Lamb, *"the Lion of the tribe of Judah, the Root of David,"*[16] we will see a half-Jew seated upon that throne, surrounded by 24 other seated Jews. Can we actually disconnect the future of the church from the future of Israel? It doesn't seem so.

So if God has been working a plan of celestial design, which He is still implementing, what is that plan?

The Family of God

We are the family of God. He fulfills His own purpose and desire by adopting us as His children and giving us His name. *"For this reason I kneel before the Father, from whom his whole family in heaven and on earth derives its name."*[17] The final outcome for us is not as clear as we would like it to be, but we know that *"now we are children of God, and what we will be has not yet been made known. But we know that when he appears, we shall be like him, for we shall see him as he is."*[18]

The redemptive role of Israel among the nations was launched to an entirely new level as Jesus the Messiah rose from the dead and the Holy Spirit was poured out upon His disciples on the Day of Pentecost. On that day, the church of Jesus Christ was empowered to carry forth the redemptive work in the earth.

---

14. Revelation 21:12.
15. Revelation 21:14.
16. Revelation 5:5.
17. Ephesians 3:14-15.
18. 1 John 3:2.

That Christ is the Master Builder and Supreme Commander of His church is beyond dispute. Jesus Himself proclaimed His ownership and superintendence of the church's construction and empowerment: *"And on this rock I will build my church, and the gates of Hades will not overcome it.""*[19] The apostle Paul declares Christ's love for and oversight of the church: *"Christ loved the church and gave himself up for her to make her holy, cleansing her by the washing with water through the word, and to present her to himself as a radiant church, without stain or wrinkle or any other blemish, but holy and blameless."*[20] He will establish her, cleanse her, make her radiant, proclaim her holy and come again for her. God is not inventing what the church is to be as it advances through human history. We can assuredly know that He is working *"according to the plan of him who works out everything in conformity with the purpose of his will."*[21] We also understand that *"He who began a good work…will carry it on to completion until the day of Christ Jesus."*[22] Just in case there is any uncertainty that God has a defined plan from the outset, He openly declares, *"'I make known the end from the beginning, from ancient times, what is still to come. I say: My purpose will stand, and I will do all that I please.'"*[23]

The church of Jesus is the eternal church that even the gates of hell cannot overcome. This is the church of power and radiance. This is the church of destiny and divine purpose. This is the church of the Firstborn, *"God's household, which is the church of the living God, the pillar and foundation of the truth."*[24]

Though Christ Himself is the Head[25] of the church and certainly knows what He is doing, it seems that we still have a great deal of misunderstanding here on earth. The confusion is

---

19. Matthew 16:18.
20. Ephesians 5:25-27.
21. Ephesians 1:11.
22. Philippians 1:6.
23. Isaiah 46:10.
24. 1 Timothy 3:15.
25. Ephesians 1:22.

clearly from the neck down. From a human perspective, there is a massive amount of disagreement as to who constitutes the church and what it should look like in its complete form. Most of the confusion about the earthly structure of the church stems from the seeming lack of detailed information in Scripture about precisely how it is to be assembled or what it will look like when completed. While perhaps it is not as detailed and specific as we would like, as we look into the New Testament, a depiction of the church of the ages begins to materialize.

The Primitive Church

The apostles of Christ who were left in charge after His Ascension began to transform the traveling evangelistic healing crusade model of ministry that Jesus gave them into a more permanent church structure. It was a process. Consider the determination of the early apostles to replace Judas after his betrayal of Jesus.[26] Not having a defined protocol for choosing apostles, they used the Old Testament method of "casting lots" to make their decision for a replacement. It is obvious that they did not yet have a final version of church structure in place. They were, in fact, experimenting.

Thankfully, the concept of choosing leadership by casting lots did not solidify into an accepted model for all ages. Some things of the past are better left in the past. It seems that the early apostles learned from their initial attempts and matured in their practices. By the time Paul and Barnabas were selected and sent into apostolic ministry, a far more reliable model for choosing leadership had developed. The consecration of Paul and Barnabas to the apostolic office was born in prayer and prophetically confirmed by the Holy Spirit.[27] It must be noted

---

26. Acts 1:15-26.
27. Acts 13:1-3.

that while the early apostles were experimenting and learning, they did rely upon the superintendence of the Holy Spirit along with their human endeavors to modify and develop the church. It should also be stated that while *they* may have been experimenting, God was not. He was, in His sovereignty, guiding their decision-making process.

In response to an unforeseen need in the Jerusalem church, the apostles originated the role of deacon.[28] Soon to follow was the institution of "elders"[29] as the church spread beyond Jerusalem. Other roles and functions developed, such as prophets, evangelists, pastors and teachers.[30] Even more ministry roles would eventually emerge, such as *"workers of miracles, also those having gifts of healing, those able to help others, those with gifts of administration and those speaking in different kinds of tongues."*[31] Located only in Jerusalem at first, the church soon began to take the Gospel to the far regions of the Roman Empire and beyond.

As the church spread, unique structures emerged. Most of these new churches maintained a strong commitment to the model of the first church in Jerusalem. But study of both the New Testament and the writings of the early church fathers reveals that there was considerable diversity in the structure of local churches and in the church at large. The development of these organizational structures was a process. Dr. Ed Hayes points out: "The New Testament gives evidence of an organized church. Like any developing institution, the church reflected the dynamism and spark of a revolution. This was not a revolution in the usual sense of total disruption, for Christianity, when it emerged, blended with its Jewish setting. However, as resistance to the message of the cross grew in intensity, the new shape of an incendiary fellowship developed. Under apostolic care and direction, organization emerged in response to necessity. This

---

28. Acts 6:1-6.
29. Acts 14:23.
30. Ephesians 4:11.
31. 1 Corinthians 12:28.

point must not be missed. From the vantage point of two thousand years later, it may seem easy for us to define the organization structures of the early church in tidy ways. Though that organization was far from tidy, patterns arose immediately after Pentecost."[32]

An accurate depiction of the church in the New Testament and the age of the early church fathers is like an architect's rendering, not a blueprint; a silhouette, not a photograph; a thumbnail sketch, not a painting.

The Church as an Architectural Rendering

Seeing the beauty and grandeur of an architectural rendering of a planned building can be an awesome experience. Not only can it help us see a dream we have had locked away in our minds, it can give us a sense of fulfillment and confidence that the dream will soon be a reality. The architect makes this experience even more special by depicting people enjoying the building, parking lots comfortably filled, trees and shrubbery lending their natural beauty to the facility and, of course, blue skies with puffy white clouds and birds in graceful flight, to add to the sensation of satisfaction and bliss.

Then the engineers and contractors arrive. Happy feelings of contentment give way to the realities of hard hats, roaring engines, piles of tangled steel, mounds of dirt and endless decisions. In moments of discouragement and apprehension we take quick peeks at the architectural rendering and encouragement begins to fill our hearts and minds again. So it is with the church.

The Bible allows us to see the church not only as it is, but as it someday will be: *"a radiant church, without stain or wrinkle or any other blemish, but holy and blameless."*[33] This beautiful

---

32. Ed Hayes, *The Church*, Word Publishing, Nashville, 1999, p. 131.
33. Ephesians 5:27.

architectural rendering pulls us forward, helping us push past the incalculable amount of details and hard work involved in actually *being* the church. But let us remember, we are not yet there. Patience with the process is of the greatest importance.

The Church as a Silhouette

As a young child, I would join my entire family on Friday evenings around the small, snowy-pictured black-and-white television screen and watch the universally popular *Alfred Hitchcock Show*. Each week would offer bizarre stories that would send a chill up your spine. Most of the programs were far too scary for a wide-eyed 6-year-old with a vivid imagination, so I did not actually watch the entire show. However, I always loved to be there for the opening. It would begin with special music and the simple sketch of a bald man with puffy cheeks and a protruding bottom lip. Then Mr. Hitchcock would step into his silhouette and begin his opening monologue. It was always thrilling to see his cartoon profile image "come alive" as he stepped into it.

Children seem to have a special fascination with shadows and silhouettes. In art class in elementary school, we carefully made construction paper cutouts of our silhouettes. These were simple outlines without details—shadows of ourselves.

As I study Scripture in regard to the New Testament church, I find a silhouette rather than a detailed picture. There is a very simple outline of the church, leaving generous room for additional details to be added. God has done this to give the church the ability to be biblically relevant in any culture, in any nation, at any point in history.

The simple "profile church" of the New Testament clearly had apostolic leadership; churches were ruled by bishops and elders; there was a council in Jerusalem convened for doctrinal debate; there were deacons, traveling prophets, evangelists and teachers; there were city-wide churches and house churches; and there was a host of cultural and language groups.

The Church as a Thumbnail Sketch

Like a masterful artist, God has put on paper a thumbnail sketch of the church in the New Testament. All of the basic elements of the final painting are present. Simple strokes denote shapes and objects that are little more than hollow images. Little time is given to careful detail at this stage. Soon, however, hollow images give way to colorful detail as light and shadows are depicted, colors are blended and texture is added. Only then is the full character of the painting revealed. So it is with the church. The basic elements have been carefully placed in Scripture. Yet it is a thumbnail sketch waiting for the materials and proper time for completion.

The heavenly Master Artist skillfully continues to add details to His church. The Holy Spirit lifts from our culture and language many things that are familiar to us, yet are still within the basic elements sketched in Scripture. The historical traditions of the church are a vital part of this mix. These additional "details" are extra-biblical but not anti-biblical. For instance, the Bible gives the word *pastor*. Little specific definition is given to the pastor's job description. To help us relate to the different ways this person may express his or her biblical calling to minister, we have created extra-biblical terms to describe this office. We have developed such titles as *senior pastor, youth pastor, co-pastor, executive pastor, assistant pastor, associate pastor, worship pastor, care pastor*…and the list goes on.

In a tribal, non-Western culture, there would be less emphasis put on the official title of *pastor* and more emphasis put on the familial title, such as *elder*. In this type of cultural setting, institutions are built around heads of families, clans and tribes. Much emphasis is given to age and tribal standing.

So which approach is right? Both titles (*pastor* and *elder*) have merit. Which one, however, is biblical? This is the complicated part—both are biblical! Each is a culturally relevant version of the basic biblical sketch. Even the way the office is carried out, no matter how it is titled, differs based on the cultural setting.

In Scripture, we find sketchy patterns for both pastors and elders. We begin to have enormous problems when we consider our own culturally relevant version of biblical church structure as something sacred that can be duplicated but never questioned, challenged or changed.

Ethnocentrism is the belief that one's own culture is superior to all others. Ethnocentricity is often the root of our determined efforts to claim our own culturally relevant version of biblical structure as the one and only "true New Testament church."

The New Testament Church

Most Christians find solace and affirmation by identifying the church to which they belong with the church of the New Testament. Since nothing else on earth rises to the level of authority of the Holy Scriptures, we correctly look to them for scriptural verification for our present-day structures. We most assuredly want to be a "New Testament church." The challenge for us is clarifying and agreeing upon exactly what *is* a New Testament church. To assert that the New Testament church was a homogeneous, smoothly functioning, clearly defined structure is simply not consistent with what we find in Scripture. What we do find is a menagerie of distinct doctrinal differences, cultural differences, strategic differences and divergent leadership personalities and styles. Many views had to be worked out over time. The pastoral offices, beginning with the apostles, had to be defined and developed. The role and requirements for Gentile believers needed debate and clarification.

We also find something in the early church that all too often is missing in our modern expressions of the church—unity of mission. Fulfillment of Christ's commission became the passion of the apostolically led church of the New Testament. Though located only in Jerusalem at first, ultimately the church broke out from its initial short-sightedness and took the Gospel to the far regions of the Roman Empire and beyond. As the church spread, unique expressions of structure emerged. Most of these new churches maintained a strong commitment to the parameters of the silhouette structure contained in the New Testament.

We each carry certain values forward from the church background from which we come. Yet when it comes to building unity in the church, we must often downplay our own preferences for the sake of cooperation. If we allow one another differences of emphasis within our own sphere of ministry, yet work hard to find points of agreement, then we have the basis of true unity and cooperation in the body of Christ. Respect of differences and belief that God is the author of these differences is central to our mutual success.

It is obvious that if God had wanted to provide a detailed pattern for all churches in all places, He could have done so. He gave very detailed instructions to Noah for construction of the ark. Even a casual study of the tabernacle or the Law of Moses clearly demonstrates God's capability and willingness to provide detailed plans to mankind. He could have given us an itemized blueprint for the church. But the church is not an inanimate object like an edifice, a boat or even a set of rules like the Law. Rather, it is a living organism, an active, breathing "body" that is able to grow, adjust to its surroundings, change its circumstances and reproduce itself.

DNA in the human body is the molecular basis of heredity. Even so, the church has a hereditary connection to God and to all of its members. Even in the most distant branches of the church, there are repeating patterns and characteristics that mysteriously reappear time after time, even if that particular branch determines to be completely distinct or separate from all others. It is as if there is a spiritual DNA within every part of the church that binds us to God's pattern, even when we do not know it or acknowledge it. By God's design, we are more alike than different, even when we go to great lengths to prove otherwise. It cannot be stated more eloquently than the words of the Holy Spirit as spoken through the apostle Paul: *"Now the body is not made up of one part but of many. If the foot should say, 'Because I am not a hand, I do not belong to the body,' it would not for that reason cease to be part of the body. And if the ear should say, 'Because I am not an eye, I do not belong to the body,' it would not for that reason cease to be part of the body. If the whole body were an eye, where would the sense of hearing be? If the whole body were an ear, where would the sense of smell be? But in fact God has arranged the parts in the body, every one of them, just as he wanted them to be. If they were all one part, where would the body be? As it is, there are many parts, but one body. The eye cannot say to the hand, 'I don't need you!' And the head cannot say to the feet, 'I don't need you!' On the contrary, those parts of the body that seem to be weaker are indispensable, and the parts that we think are less honorable we treat with special honor. And the parts that are unpresentable are treated with special modesty, while our presentable parts need no special treatment. But God has combined the members of the body and has given greater honor to the parts that lacked it, so that there should be no division in the body, but that its parts should have equal concern for each other. If one part suffers, every part suffers with it; if one part is honored, every part rejoices with it.*[34]

No division in the body. Lord, in Your mercy, make it so in this generation.

Key Discussion Points:

1. God's eternal plan for the people of God, His family.
2. The church as an architect's rendering, a silhouette and a thumbnail sketch.
3. The Church as a living organism, able to adjust, change and reproduce.
4. The DNA of the church.

Questions:

1. Does your church or denomination have a unity of purpose and continuity with the early church?
2. Do you agree or disagree that the different Christian denominations have more in common than not?

---

34. 1 Corinthians 12:14-26.

Chapter Four

⸻ ∞ ⸻

The Church Universal

The Visible and Invisible Church

⸻ ∞ ⸻

J esus prayed in John 17:11, *"And now I am no more in the world, but these are in the world, and I come to thee. Holy Father, keep through thine own name those whom thou hast given me, that they may be one, as we are."* (KJV) He continues: *"'My prayer is not for them alone. I pray also for those who will believe in me through their message, that all of them may be one, Father, just as you are in me and I am in you. May they also be in us so that the world may believe that you have sent me. I have given them the glory that you gave me, that they may be one as we are one: I in them and you in me. May they be brought to complete unity to let the world know that you sent me and have loved them even as you have loved me.'"*[1] This intercessory prayer of Jesus is still suspended in the heavenlies, resulting in a spiritual unity that only God Himself can bring.

---

1. John 17:20-23.

Organizational unity in the church seems impossible. But organic unity is absolutely necessary. Though our connection to one another is as deep as DNA, we do seem quite different.

We are one family, one body, one blood, but *many* parts. To finish the work Christ gave us will require unprecedented cooperation. But when we survey the Christian world and see so many distinct denominations, it is difficult to believe that we will ever achieve cooperative unity.

An understanding of the philosophy behind the formation of denominations helps us see how they have the potential to bring us together instead of keep us apart. Consider the following comments offered by Dr. Bruce L. Shelley: "Denominations, as originally designed, are the opposite of sectarianism. A sect claims the authority of Christ for itself alone. It believes that it is the true Body of Christ; all truth belongs to it and to no other religion. So by definition, a sect is exclusive. The word 'denomination' by contrast was an inclusive term. It implied that the Christian group called or 'denominated' by a particular name was but one member of a larger group—the Church—to which all denominations belong. The denominational theory of the Church, then, insists that the true Church cannot be identified with any single ecclesiastical structure. No denomination claims to represent the whole Church of Christ. Each simply constitutes a different form—in worship and organization—of the larger life of the Church."[2] Further insight on the "denominational theory" is offered by Dr. Rex Koivisto: "A denominational theory of the church treats all Christian groupings, even the most ancient or the largest, on an equal footing. They are all but parts (denominations) of the entire catholic "church." They have no greater, nor lesser claim to be called "church" than any other grouping of genuine Christians. Nor should they expect other Christian groupings to come and merge or be subsumed by them.

---

2. Bruce L. Shelley, *Church History in Plain Language*, Word Publishing, Dallas, Texas, 1982, 1985, p. 306.

Understanding this can lead to a broader fundamental paradigm shift in our thinking toward a broader catholicity."[3]

If this philosophy presented by Shelley and Koivisto were broadly agreed upon and accepted, it would give us bridges to unity instead of denominations presenting walls, as is often the case. Recognizing that we are but a *part* of a larger *whole* is a beginning point for genuine unity and cooperation. The communication and organizational structures of denominations, as well as their education and media power, could provide needed systems of fostering unity and strategic cooperation. I once heard Dr. Paul Cedar proclaim to a huge auditorium filled with leaders from every segment of the church from around the world: "Denominations are not dead; denominationalism is dead."[4] There was thunderous applause; we each understood precisely what he meant. Denominations simply represent distinctives. Denominationalism signifies sectarianism. Denominations can exist without sectarianism, while retaining their structural autonomy, preferences and distinct characteristics.

While we can learn to appreciate the value of denominations functioning separately, we cannot give up on the idea of greater *visible* unity in the church. Though our strongest connection to one another is the *invisible*, greater visible unity is vital to revealing God's full nature to the world around us and to accomplishing all that He desires of us on the earth.

Some of the present-day confusion about the singular nature of the church comes from a lack of understanding of its invisible quality. When we speak of the "invisible church," we portend that what makes us **"the church of the living God, the pillar and foundation of the truth"**[5] cannot be perceived with

---

3. Rex A. Koivisto, *One Lord, One Faith,* Victor Books/SP Publications, Inc., Wheaton, Illinois, 1993, p. 105.
4. This statement by Dr. Paul Cedar was made in a general assembly speech to approximately ten thousand mission leaders from around the world in 1995 at the Global Consultation on World Evangelism.
5. 1 Timothy 3:15.

human senses. In other words, it is invisible. Colossians 1:16 reveals that there are both concrete and invisible aspects to God and His creation: *"For by him all things were created; things in heaven and on earth, visible and invisible, whether thrones or powers or rulers or authorities; all things were created by him and for him."* St. Augustine's description of a sacrament as "an outward and visible sign of an inward and spiritual grace" also speaks to the invisible qualities of the kingdom of God. The invisible is as real as the visible, and in some cases even more genuine. Christ Himself binds us together by the Holy Spirit. It is not a visible church structure or particular form of worship that defines us as His church.

The "visible church" as seen through our human structures is imperfect and not, in itself, sufficient. The great Presbyterian theologian William Cunningham stated, "The visible has in men's minds, to a large extent, swallowed up the invisible church, or thrown it into the background; and men have come, to a large extent, to judge practicality of what the Church of Christ should be by what it too often, in its eternal aspects, actually is."[6] We must, therefore, guard against placing too much emphasis on the external expression of the invisible church.

While it is true that much of what makes us the church is invisible, God has always maintained a visible community on the earth. Israel was chosen to be the "people of God" and to be a testimony to all nations. The church continues this testimony as the "family of believers." We are God's family. We are Christ's body: *"Christ is the head of the church, his body, of which he is the Savior."*[7] Jesus saved us from destruction by redeeming us as a community, not as a collection of individuals. There is a mystical connection between Christ our Head and His church on the earth. Dr. Robert Webber states: "Paul's reference to the Church as the Body of Christ is therefore not

---

6. William Cunningham, *Historical Theology*, The Bath Press, Avon, Scotland, 1862, p. 26.
7. Ephesians 5:23.

a mere metaphor containing social and psychological value, but a statement about the relationship that exists between Christ and His Body. It says that Christ is one with the Church, that the existence of the Church is an essential continuation of the life of Jesus in the world; the Church is a divine creation which, in a mystical yet real way, co-inheres with the Son who is made present through it."[8]

We have a collective role as the expression of Christ's body in the earth. In a very tangible way, we are God's face to the world.

A mother was tucking her 5-year-old son, Aaron, into bed when he asked, "Mommy, what is God like?" She pondered for a moment and answered, "Well sweetheart, God is love." He looked at her quizzically and asked, "What does God's face look like?" "I suppose He looks like love," she replied. A big grin beamed from the little boy's face as he excitedly announced, "Mommy, I know what God's face looks like, He looks like you!"

You see, once little Aaron understood the nature of God, he could see God's face in his mother's. So it is with the church. When we in collective unity demonstrate God's love, the world can begin to see His face through us. Yet there is more. Though we as the body of Christ present to the world a tangible expression of the face of God, it is a face with many expressions. There is unity, but not uniformity. No human organization on earth is more diverse than the church of Jesus Christ.

One of the marvels of the visible and invisible nature of the church is its multiplicity of expression. Scripture uses many metaphors to define the church. We are likened to a body that has many parts.[9] We are described as a building that is being assembled,[10] the family of believers[11] and the household of God.[12] As is the case with all families, each individual member is

---

8. Robert E. Webber, *Ancient-Future Faith*, Baker Books, Grand Rapids, Michigan, 1999, p. 81.
9. 1 Corinthians 12:12.
10. Ephesians 2:19-22.
11. Galatians 6:10.
12. 1 Timothy 3:15.

unique, but we are all universally bound together by blood and by name.[13] As with a human body, the church has parts that are so different it is sometimes difficult to see how they fit together, yet they do.

Buildings are an amazing collection of distinct materials, yet when the materials are brought together in thoughtful assembly, there is strength, beauty and functionality. The same is true of the church. We have many unique expressions, many different streams, yet we are one collective river that roars with diversity and might. In Psalm 46:4 we read, *"There is a river whose streams make glad the city of God, the holy place where the Most High dwells."* There are different streams, yet they flow into one river that pleases the throngs of heaven and, more important, pleases the One who is seated upon the throne. God is the designer of His church and the author of its diversity. It has separate parts, but a universal nature.

The Church Catholic

This universal nature of the church is the basis of our "catholicity." Just using the words *catholic* or *catholicity* in many Christian circles is inflammatory. The word *catholic* refers to the "universal church" and should not be confused with any specific branch of the church that uses it as part of its name. For the first one thousand years of church history, there was simply no other commonly used term to describe the universal nature of the church. The word *catholic* is still commonly used in many branches of the church to describe our invisible and visible connections to Christ as our Head and to one another as brothers and sisters in Christ.

It would surprise most Christians to discover just how catholic they actually are. Catholicity begins with our entry into the body of Christ through our spiritual rebirth and baptism.

---

13. Ephesians 3:14-15.

The apostle Paul brings this issue of catholicity to the forefront when he asserts, *"so in Christ we who are many form one body, and each member belongs to all the others."*[14] And again: *"For we were all baptized by one Spirit into one body—whether Jews or Greeks, slave or free—and we were all given the one Spirit to drink. Now the body is not made up of one part but of many."*[15] The Nicene Creed boldly declares, "We believe in one holy catholic and apostolic church." Catholicity is both biblical and historical.

A truly catholic view of the church is one of comprehensiveness, not exclusiveness; embracing, not parochial; openhearted, not sectarian. It requires an acknowledgment and acceptance of God's ordained diversity within His body. Meekness and humility characterize it, not arrogance or elitism. Its leaders seek to understand and discern rather than adjudicate and censor. Catholicity is further expressed by identifying with the ancient, undivided, universal Christian church and carrying forward historical continuity from it.

In the second century, catholicity took on another aspect of meaning beyond the universal church. Catholicity began to be identified with orthodoxy. After assaults from heresies such as Gnosticism and Arianism, the early church fathers saw a need to establish a baseline of beliefs for the whole church. By the fourth century, the church found it necessary to find biblically legitimate "creeds" upon which Christians could depend. The creeds in simpler forms had emerged early in the primitive church, but were universally accepted in the same time frame as the canonization of the Holy Scriptures. The creeds were not intended to replace or supercede the canonized Scriptures. They were created to establish simple, scripturally based standards of tenets for the church. The Apostles' Creed and the Nicene Creed have historically been recognized as containing the primary body of beliefs necessary for orthodox Christianity.

---

14. Romans 12:5.
15. 1 Corinthians 12:13,14.

It is to their own harm that some branches of the church have moved away from teaching their members these important creeds. The result has often been unchecked extremism or even heresy. Catholicity without orthodoxy is incomplete and potentially dangerous. The creeds have held a prominent place of importance throughout history, and have served to protect the church from doctrinal extremism and reinforce genuine catholicity,

So catholicity has both a "unity expression" and an "orthodoxy expression." Both are needed for true catholicity.

As in relationships within a family, the practice of biblical catholicity requires prayer, love, faith, commitment and care with words. Since we are so different from one another, yet bound to one another, a strong commitment to endure through the differences is required. There is no substitute for time together. Patience must be allowed to finish its work of maturity and completion.[16] Christians today have a high need and desire to gather together in affinity groups. These gatherings, whether they are prayer groups, Bible studies or activity fellowships, are growing in number and are typically cross-denominational in nature. The most remarkable aspect of this trend among Christians is that even pastors and leaders are hungering for more "affinity contact" with other leaders, while in the recent past they tended to stay within their own denominational associations for fellowship. Perhaps this propensity to cross barriers for fellowship simply reflects cultural change, or perhaps it is part of God's divine plan working us toward His stated intent of unity in the church. Could that be the sound of rushing waters I hear softly rumbling behind this trend?

In Ephesians 5:25-27 we read, *"Christ loved the church and gave himself up for her to make her holy, cleansing her by the washing with water through the word, and to present her to himself as a radiant church, without stain or wrinkle or any*

---

16. James 1:4.

other blemish, but holy and blameless." We, too, must love her. One of the highest forms of love is expressed as we pray for others. Sometimes, while traveling, I pull into the parking lot of a local church and pray for it. I pray for its pastor and leadership. I pray for its openness to the Holy Spirit and the Word of God. I pray that its mission and vision will be accomplished. It actually increases the quality of my prayer that I know little or nothing about this particular local church. I have found that as I pray for different expressions of the church universal, and guard my tongue when I speak of its diversity, that my love for it increases. Prayer may be the most practical method for developing a baseline of catholicity and effective cooperation. Praying with others opens the heart to God and to them. It is very difficult to maintain prejudices against those with whom we pray.

I have been privileged to participate in cross-denominational prayer in many different settings. Even the most innocuous, bland and spiritless pastors' prayer gatherings in which I have participated helped me to be more acknowledging of the sincerity of others from divergent theological and worship preferences. While regularly participating in cross-denominational prayer of the lackluster variety, where everyone is overly cautious to not offend, my true passion is to pray with other leaders who are aggressively seeking unity in the church that we may be agents of transformation of the world around us. For the past few years, I have been a part of a group of pastors and leaders who gather to pray for our region. We pray in weekly, quarterly and annual gatherings. This is not prayer of the namby-pamby variety. This is heartfelt, desperate, passionate intercession for one another and for our region, that it might be transformed for Christ. Deep relationships and effective cooperation have grown out of this cross-denominational and cross-racial prayer movement. Recently, one of the participating pastors who is new to the group enthusiastically gushed, "I love to pray with men and women who *need* to pray." That's it. Praying for catholicity is not an option; it is a necessity.

To walk in catholicity requires faith in God's sovereignty in His church. Even in branches of His church that seem cold, filled with mixture or apostate, as in the days of Elijah,[17] God sovereignly reserves to Himself those who sincerely serve Him. Dr. Peter C. Moore suggests that catholicity compels this confession: "We confess that, despite corruption and frequent error, the historic Church is nonetheless God's Church."[18]

Additionally, we must not conclude that we are the only ones who are truly serving God today. The burning flame of life is still evident in every diverse expression of the church. There are always those who refuse to surrender to anything less than passionate love for Christ and dedicated obedience to His will, yet we, like the prophet Elijah, can get into such a state of delusion that we come to feel as he did: "*I have been very zealous for the LORD God Almighty.... I am the only one left, and now they are trying to kill me too.*"[19] As it turned out, the Lord had preserved for Himself many others who were faithful to Him, even while Elijah, the devoted man of God, was wholly unaware of them.

Many times, we do not recognize the faithfulness of others within the various branches of the church outside of our own precisely because we are so focused on our conspicuous differences. Perhaps our ignorance can also be attributed to unwillingness on our part to research what God has done or may be doing among others outside of our stream. Is it possible that we are comfortable with our prejudices, and that we are simply unwilling to investigate whether what we think about Christians from different streams is, in fact, accurate? Sweeping, generalized opinions of others allow us to continue in our cozy biases, and permit us the comfort of never needing to inquire, think deeply or reexamine our opinions.

---

17. 1 Kings 19:14-18.
18. Peter C. Moore, *A Church to Believe In*, Latimer Press, Bainbridge, Ohio, 1994, p. 50.
19. 1 Kings 19:14.

We have become so accustomed to division and broken-ness that it now seems normal. Since God Himself is the creator of diversity, it is reasonable to accept and value the differences and unique expressions within the body of Christ, the church of the Firstborn. But while much good comes from our diversity, is division necessary? Can we be distinct without divorcing ourselves from one another? Is God pleased with the rancor, judgmentalism and outright rejection of validity that so often characterizes the branches of the church?

Catholicity, above all else, requires humility. Like all relationship building, catholicity demands that we first respect the other person by demonstrating a willingness to lay down our own preferences. Essentials of faith cannot be compromised, not even for the sake of unity, but what we consider to be essentials of the faith often are nothing more than our own preferences.

The differences and even deceptions that are often so obvious make it difficult to stay in faith, deeming that the prayer of Jesus that we will be "one" will come to pass. This is where commitment to catholicity comes into play. We must fully commit ourselves to believe for complete unity in the church. Our belief must be consistently expressed in actions that demonstrate the faith and commitment we possess. We must keep in mind that unity is not an option; it is a command. To be committed to unity is to be committed to the will of God. It is to be surrendered to God's plan.

Careful Consideration in Nomenclatures

Words are often the demise of unity. "Nomenclature" is a system or set of terms used in a given discipline, such as art, science or religion. Nothing more effectively unravels our unity than the careless use of nomenclature. In our human efforts to understand and explain spiritual things, we create terminology by which we identify truth. We then confidently expect everyone else to simply understand and agree with our jargon. More often than not, the nomenclature we use to emphasize our views is extra-biblical, yet we give it the same level of reverence as biblical terminology. Many avoidable problems have begun this way.

"Avoid terminology that is identified with controversy." This was the advice of my late spiritual father, Costa Deir. It came during one of my "woodshed moments," when he, like a true father in the faith, graciously but directly confronted an area of failure in my life. He had actually diverted his planned trip to Brazil to visit me in Ecuador. He had never done anything of this nature before, so I knew there was a serious issue he wanted to address. To this day, I do not know how he even became aware of the problem, but his desire to protect me from self-defeating, leadership-undermining behaviors was great.

I was embroiled in a controversy in which we felt we were being accused of teaching things that, in fact, we were not teaching. At the center of the tempest was terminology that a visiting teacher to our Bible school had used in class. Emotions had been stirred, attacks and counterattacks had been made, and interest in understanding what actually had been said or meant had long since been abandoned. We felt so hurt by what we considered unfair treatment that we greatly increased the magnitude of the problem by inappropriate and ill-advised responses. The whole situation became like Brer Rabbit and the Tar Baby in the famous story *Song of the South*. The more we tried to distance ourselves from the dilemma, the more stuck to it we became. In time, the whole affair just slipped away into the distant past, but was never actually resolved.

The wisdom of Costa's counsel became abundantly clear— avoid the controversy in the first place by exercising care in our choice of words. In other words, *"keep a tight rein on [your] tongue."*[20] Dad's concern for me was not just this isolated incident, but, as always, that my actions henceforth would be those of a careful man. His deep concern underscored for me how

---

20. James 1:26.

important it is to be intentional with our words and behavior when they impact others.

Words are powerful. However, they are not standardized. They convey different meanings to different people. Take the word *denominational* for instance. To a pastor within a group that considers itself Christ-centered, biblical and ordained by God, this word represents tremendous good. To declare a pastor "denominational" would, in this case, be considered a compliment. But with the secularization and decline of some denominations and the onset of vast numbers of highly independent, nondenominational churches, we have a new use for the word *denominational*. It is most often used among independents as a synonym for *apostate, humanistic, controlling* and *irrelevant to what God is doing on the earth today*. Other adjectives often accompany the word *denominational*, such as *dead* or *traditional*. Many nondenominational pastors have become cynical and their words caustic, including phrases such as "God's frozen chosen." Some of this rancor began as a result of the rejection and abuse many experienced within the very denominations they now criticize. Many independents were ousted from their denominations because their innovations or their personal spiritual experiences were not acceptable to the status quo. The acrimonious use of the words *independent* or *nondenominational* by the denominational pastors also helped breed the attitude that now is manifest in those who use *denominational* as a put-down. Clearly, there is wrong on both sides of this situation.

We cannot change the past, but we can change the future. Considering the new climate of unity and cooperation that is moving throughout the body of Christ, we should work even harder to use care with words that potentially cause division. We must choose terminology that does not separate or cause unneeded offense. Yes, extremes and serious problems do exist in denominations and in independent nondenominational churches. Nevertheless, we must be careful not to paint an entire movement or branch of the "one holy catholic and apostolic church" with a single broad brush.

We can each remain true to our convictions while using care with our words. In fact, the Bible admonishes us to do so. Colossians 4:6 states, *"Let your conversation be always full of grace, seasoned with salt, so that you may know how to answer everyone."* We should always attempt to qualify the words we use to describe others and be sure they are seasoned with grace and pure motives. Otherwise, we will suffer in our relationships with others—and we will be judged by God: *"'But I tell you that men will have to give account on the day of judgment for every careless word they have spoken. For by your words you will be acquitted, and by your words you will be condemned.'"*[21] As God gives us grace to heal cultural and racial divisions, denominational breaches and the other separations that remain, we must commit ourselves to make our words part of the healing process.

In Romans 15:7 we read, *"Accept one another, then, just as Christ accepted you, in order to bring praise to God."* This simple yet profound statement is one of the most basic requirements in the church. We each hold dear our own ideals of doctrinal correctness and proper church structure. This is the way it must be. Without ideals, without high standards, we will not rise to the place of excellence and commitment that Christ demands. Normally, we realize that our own goals and ideals are higher than we presently experience. Therefore, we allow for God's grace to cover us until we reach the mark for which we are aiming. Yet when we consider other local churches or denominations that seem to have different ideals or doctrine, we do not allow them this same grace on which we understandably depend. This is a double standard and no doubt displeasing to God, who expects us to judge others with the same measure we judge ourselves. I once heard someone say: "For every point of view, there are many points of deception." Self-deception is the most insidious strain of deception. A high potential for self-deception occurs when we prematurely judge

---

21. Matthew 12:36-37.

the points of view of others as wrong, while ignoring the possibility that we ourselves could be in error.

Why are we so ready to jump to the conclusion that others' motives are not pure, and therefore judge them undeserving of God's grace to grow? Simply stated, it is because we do not accept them as valid brethren. We judge others by their actions, but we judge ourselves by our motives. We believe we have good motives, so if we slip along the way, we forgive ourselves because we know that we really *meant* well. After all, occasionally, *hasta el mejor mono se le cae el banano* (even the best monkey will drop the banana). This is fine, but we must extend to others this same grace. Catholicity requires that we consider other parts of the body of Christ as valid brethren and convey this conviction with our words and attitudes.

God Himself is the designer and builder of this marvelously diverse entity that is His church. We must learn to embrace it and celebrate it in all its diversity, just as He does. To be truly catholic, one cannot disclaim connection to any part of God's true church, no matter how it has disappointed, behaved badly or failed to rise to perfection. It is required that we abandon all demands for uniformity of styles and perceptions, trusting God to help us *"keep the unity of the Spirit through the bond of peace."*[22]

And any attempt to embrace this level of unity will fail if it is not done by the power of the cross. Only as we fully embrace our death to self can we live together in true harmony.

One of the most outstanding features of the heavenly city will be its splendid walls, which will demonstrate God's limitless provision and surrounding strength. But while God builds walls of protection around His people,[23] we constantly erect walls of division within His church. The apostle Paul petitions, *"I appeal to you, brothers, in the name of our Lord Jesus Christ, that all of you agree with one another so that there may be no divisions*

---

22. Ephesians 4:3.
23. See Ezra 9:9; Job 1:10.

among you and that you may be perfectly united in mind and thought."[24] No divisions? Perfectly united in mind and thought? These seem like lofty goals for the universal church, or even for a single local congregation. We must not, however, lose sight of what is possible. Jesus would not have prayed for our unity if it were not possible. For God, the impossible is normal, commonplace. We can take heart in Christ's promise: *"'With man this is impossible, but with God all things are possible.'"*[25]

We must, then, be genuinely catholic in our attitudes and actions toward the body of Christ, His holy and beloved church, for which Christ Jesus gave His all. The church has an invisible quality that binds us to God through the Holy Spirit, yet we also are a visible community that proclaims a testimony of God. The church is truly apostolic only when it recognizes its universality, its catholicity.

Yesterday, Today and Forever

There is a *"yesterday, today and forever"*[26] nature in the church that cascades downward from Jesus the Head. The church cannot be fully understood outside of the context of its history, present and eternal future. Focusing only upon the contemporary church, or just the church of the New Testament, will leave significant gaps in our understanding.

Many Christians are aware that the church has a history of two thousand years, but they do not see much significance in its past, concluding that there is no true value in understanding church history. They have little interest in the significant gap of time between the 70 or so years of the New Testament and the church of today.

Some years ago I had the privilege of taking the 30-day "Perspectives on the World Christian Movement" course offered

---

24. 1 Corinthians 1:10.
25. Matthew 19:26.
26. Hebrews 13:8.

through William Carey University. What an uncommon "whole body of Christ" experience that was for me on the campus of the U.S. Center for World Evangelization in Pasadena, California. Every day we studied with brothers and sisters from across the spectrum of the church and from around the world. Every age, education and socioeconomic level was represented. How beautiful and captivating the body of Christ can be!

One of the classes in Pasadena introduced me to the "BOBO Theory," developed by Dr. Ralph Winter. "BOBO" is an acronym for "blink off, blink on." Many believers suffer from this common ailment. The BOBO Theory is characterized by the tendency to think that what is really important about church history "blinked off" about the time of the death of the original apostles. Then, just before we personally come to Christ, history blinks back on again. To a person suffering from this malady, everything that happened during those approximately nineteen hundred intervening years is simply irrelevant.

On this subject of continuity and generation-to-generation connectivity, Bishop Lesslie Newbigin states: "The Reformers have given us an intensely dynamic conception of the Church. They took with immense seriousness the truth that the Church is the body of Christ, that He is ever dynamically creative in it and through it, that He, the living Lord, is in very truth present today in His Church through the word and the sacraments with power to create and re-create, to convert and to reconcile, to root up and pull down, to build and to plant. The obvious defect of this conception, as it has manifested itself in the subsequent centuries of Protestant development, is that it gives no real place to the continuing life of the Church as one fellowship binding the generations together in Christ. It makes of the Church practically a series of totally disconnected events in which, at each moment and place at which the word and sacraments are set forth, the Church is there and then called into being by God's creative power."[27]

---

27. Lesslie Newbigin, *The Household of God*, Paternoster Press, London, first published 1953 (SCM Press Ltd.), reprinted 1998, p. 57.

The sense of disconnection that Bishop Newbigin describes has many subtle and profound effects upon us. Thus, when a connection can be made, there is typically a flood of positive results. Notice Dr. Robert Webber's enthusiasm as he describes this experience: "To affirm our identity with all of God's people everywhere is to recover from historical amnesia and to discover our identity. We belong to a great company of saints. We can claim Augustine, Aquinas, Luther, Calvin, Wesley, and Moody as our ancestors. We belong to them and they to us. Together we are one in Jesus Christ our Head. Thanks be to God!"[28]

In addition to the lack of historical connection and continuity caused by the BOBO Syndrome, many are plagued by excessive individualism. Heaven is not a collection of individuals; it is a *community of faith*. Christ's church is a citizenry of faith with connection and continuity from the time of the apostles throughout eternity. Our modern tendency toward extreme individualism makes viewing the church as a community difficult. Dr. Gordon Fee speaks to one of the challenges we face in these modernistic and humanistic days as he addresses individualism: "One of the sure members of the modern world's 'trinity,' along with relativism and secularism, is individualism. Recapturing the biblical significance of the individual, but revising it to fit a non-biblical, naturalistic worldview, the Enlightenment led the modern Western world into a totally individualistic understanding of life, which has never been more prevalent than it is today. The individual is the be-all and the end-all of everything; subservience of individual rights to the common good has become the new 'heresy' to be rejected at all cost."[29] This lack of connection to the community, along with the lack of accountability that this generates, has led to many problems at every level of the church.

---

28. Robert E. Webber, *Evangelicals on the Canterbury Trail*, Morehouse Publishing, Harrisburg, Pa., 1985, p. 66.
29. Gordon D. Fee, *Paul, the Spirit, and the People of God*, Peabody, Massachusetts, 1996, p. 64.

With the breakdown of connections comes a breakdown of commitments, which ultimately leads to a breakdown of ethical behavior. If I have no responsibility to the community, then I can do as I please and proclaim irrefutable divine right as an individual child of God to do it. Now, even highly recognized Christian leaders simply do as they personally will, no matter how outrageous the behavior, and claim God bestowed sovereignty to continue their conduct and remain in public ministry without concern for how it affects the body of Christ or our mission to the world. Understanding the church to be a community of faith, the people of God, is vital to experiencing the protective restraints that it offers. Dr. Fee continues: "Though entered individually, salvation is seldom if ever thought of as a one-on-one relationship with God. While such a relationship is included, to be sure, 'to be saved' means especially to be joined to the people of God. In this sense, the third century church father Cyprian had it right: there is no salvation outside the church because God is saving a *people* for His name, not a miscellaneous, unconnected set of individuals."

The church of Jesus Christ is a continuing community of faith that has endured throughout history, lives today and will remain forever in heaven. As is Jesus, so is the church: yesterday, today and forever. *"But you have come to Mount Zion, to the heavenly Jerusalem, the city of the living God. You have come to thousands upon thousands of angels in joyful assembly, to the church of the firstborn, whose names are written in heaven. You have come to God, the judge of all men, to the spirits of righteous men made perfect."*[30] So the church is not only a contemporary community of testimony, it is a "continuing community" that has a past, present and future role in God's global plan, as well as our individual lives.

The church may seem imperfect from an earthly perspective, but we can definitely be sure of this one thing—God is building His church and we can trust His work. That God would

---

30. Hebrews 12:22-23.

allow us to be such an active part of this process is indeed a mystery. Yet I find it easy to trust that everything will come together in the final analysis. After all, the Creator, God and Father of all we survey, clearly knows what He is doing as He establishes us as His community of faith, the people of God.

Key Discussion Points:

1. The visible and invisible natures of the church.
2. Understanding and fostering catholicity.
3. Care with words in cross-denominational relationships.
4. The nature of Christ's church as a continuing community of faith and the value of historical connections.

Questions:

1. Are you careful with your "nomenclatures" or is there room for improvement? How so?
2. What are your thoughts with regard to the idea that denominations are not inherently bad, but, in fact, simply represent distinctions of the universal church?
3. Do you have a catholic view of the church?
4. What does that mean to you?
5. Can you describe ways that you would like to see the church demonstrate greater visible unity?

Chapter Five

❦

The Apostolic Church

The Advent of Apostolic Ministry

A community of faith must have recognized leadership or it eventually will turn into a listless mob. Since God's will for His church is not that it simply be *present* in the earth but that it act upon His command to take the message of Christ *"to every creature,"* Jesus established an order of leadership along with the mission He gave. This new order of leadership for the people of God launched forward with the appointment and commissioning of the first apostles.

We find in the New Testament that, after a night of prayer, Jesus hand-selected (and subsequently trained) a group of "special messengers" who would become His ministry associates, and later, part of *"the foundation"*[1] upon which He would build His church. Considering the important role that these men would one day fulfill, it is no wonder that He approached these appointments with such prayerful consideration. Jesus

---

1. Ephesians 2:20.

one day would delegate the foundational authority of His church to these men. They would guide the church through its infancy and leave an extraordinary legacy and testimony of Christ that would endure throughout the ages. And they would become the first link in a successive chain of apostolic leadership and ministry. No decision could have been more crucial to the future of the church than the appointments that Jesus made that day.

These carefully chosen apostles were commissioned to service and ministry at Jesus' side. They listened to His teachings, watched His daily life and received personal discipleship from the Master. He sent them out to preach and conferred upon them the power to perform miracles in His name. They were brought into direct partnership with the Master and His earthly ministry very quickly, and the full weight of the ministry of Christ would soon fall upon them. As Daniel-Ropps stated it: "The philosophers of Greece and the prophets of Israel, including the Baptist, all had their professed disciples, but none of these was invested with the power and authority of the master. The schools of Stoic philosophy, for instance, consisted of individuals animated by the same ideals but working independently. Only the neo-Pythagoreans had anything like a rudimentary hierarchy. But the Church of Christ was hardly born before it found its leaders."[2] Their "on-the-job-training" with Jesus would straightaway become invaluable.

By all accounts, these were not perfect men. They themselves left us the written record of their lives in what became Holy Scripture, not attempting to gloss over their foibles or failures. As we read what was inspired by God, but penned by men, the apostles seem amazingly comfortable, under the guidance of the Holy Spirit, to reveal that their personal growth and the development of the church was a process.

---

2. Daniel-Ropps, *Jesus and His Times*, E.P. Dutton & Co., Inc., New York, 1954, p. 279.

"They were indeed godly men, who had shown the sincerity of their piety by forsaking all for their Master's sake. But at the time of their call they were exceedingly ignorant, narrow-minded, superstitious, full of Jewish prejudices, misconceptions and animosities. They had much to learn of what was bad, as well as much to unlearn of what was good, and they were slow to learn and unlearn."[3] But while they were flawed men, their dedication to Christ and the empowering on the Holy Spirit after the Day of Pentecost combined to bring them swiftly to a place of spiritual maturity and preparation for the next phase of their work—the development of the New Testament church.

After Jesus' ascension to heaven, the apostles became the principal source for the stories and teachings of Christ in the primitive church. Their prior close association with the Savior and the continuing revelation of the Holy Spirit empowered them with unique knowledge. As the apostle John himself stated, *"Jesus did many other things as well. If every one of them were written down, I suppose that even the whole world would not have room for the books that would be written."*[4] They began to produce written accounts of what they had seen and heard, and also sent teaching letters to the emerging churches. These written accounts and letters were canonized as Scripture in the fourth century.

The apostles became a part of the very foundation of the church with Jesus Himself being the "chief cornerstone": *"Consequently, you are no longer foreigners and aliens, but fellow citizens with God's people and members of God's household, built on the foundation of the apostles and prophets, with Christ Jesus himself as the chief cornerstone."*[5]

---

3. A.B. Bruce, *The Training of the Twelve*, Kregel Publications, Grand Rapids, Michigan, 1971, p. 14. Reproduced from the Fourth Edition, Revised and Improved, 1894 by A.C. Armstrong and Son.

4. John 21:25.

5. Ephesians 2:19-20.

Apostolic Tradition and Succession

At the end of the first century, Clement of Rome (Clemens Romanus) described the essence of apostolic tradition and succession: "The apostles received the Gospel for us from the Lord Jesus Christ; Jesus the Christ was sent from God. Thus Christ is from God, the Apostles from Christ: in both cases the process was orderly, and derived from the will of God."[6] By this statement, Clement proclaimed the legitimacy of Christ's earthly ministry and showed how God established a recognizable order of succession for the apostolic ministry. Distinct aspects of apostolic ministry emerged as the early apostles carried forth the ministry of Christ into the church and the world, and can be evaluated in two ways: apostolic tradition and apostolic succession.

Apostolic Tradition

The practices and teachings of the apostles, recorded in Scripture and subsequently in the writings of the early church fathers, can be described as the "traditions of the apostles." The apostles became the source of the message and ongoing ministry of Christ because, as Clement stated, "The apostles received the Gospel for us from the Lord Jesus Christ." This set of practices and teachings can also be described as the "apostolic faith." These "traditions" give us a model for apostolic ministry. The apostolic tradition is one of orthodox teaching (*"They devoted themselves to the apostles' teaching."*[7]) confirmed by expansion of the church through evangelism (*"With great power the apostles continued to testify to the resurrection of the Lord Jesus, and much grace was with them all."*[8]) and through demonstration of the supernatural (*"The things that*

---

6. Henry Bettenson, *The Early Christian Fathers*, Oxford University Press, Oxford, 1956, p. 32.
7. Acts 2:42.
8. Acts 4:33.

mark an apostle—signs, wonders and miracles—were done among you with great perseverance."[9]). The combination of devotion to scriptural orthodoxy and spirit-empowered ministry is the essence of apostolic tradition as we are defining it here.

Without functional apostolic tradition, attempts to exercise a form of apostolic oversight or ministry in the universal church degrade into mere administrative work or inappropriate human control. There are far too many historic and contemporary examples of leaders who have the authority of their office without the anointing and spiritual fruit necessary to bring forth genuine apostolic ministry.

It can be rightfully argued that anyone who follows the teachings of the apostles through Scripture, and does the works of the apostles outlined therein, is, in fact, following in the tradition and faith of the early apostles. This would constitute continuity with the *tradition* of the apostles, though it could not be considered an unbroken succession of their bestowed authority. We will now look at how this authority is passed along.

Apostolic Succession

The authority line of the early apostles was preserved by "setting apart" or "ordaining" their successors by the laying on of hands.[10] Jesus commissioned the first apostles by the laying on of hands, and they continued this form of commissioning into the primitive church and beyond.

These successors were carefully chosen. There was an orderly succession of authority passed on to others who were called to carry forth the apostolic ministry. They were appointed by the apostles and their successors, not elected or self-appointed. This continuity of authority through succession can be reliably traced back to at least the second century

---

9. 2 Corinthians 12:12.
10. Acts 13:1-3; Titus 1:5.

through the consecration of bishops. This is the essence of historic "apostolic succession."

These early apostles had universally recognized authority, and they dealt straightforwardly with those who had a spirit of independence (*"I wrote to the church, but Diotrephes, who loves to be first, will have nothing to do with us. So if I come, I will call attention to what he is doing."*[11]) or with those who preached false doctrine (*"As I urged you…stay there in Ephesus so that you may command certain men not to teach false doctrines any longer.*[12]). They also began to bring order to the church to complement its powerful anointing.

Whether one accepts the desirability of "an unbroken chain of succession" or not, we can clearly see that there has been some form of authoritative succession from the earliest biblical record of the church. Even churches that begin independent from any other line of succession initiate some order of authority and commissioning as they raise up leadership, ministries and congregations.

One might ask, "How is it possible to recognize the apostolic succession of authority when it appears that, at times, those passing along that authority may have done it with wrong motives, or were seemingly apostate?" The answer is as simple as this: Bishops can no more destroy the validity of their office than any Christian can destroy the power of the Gospel.

The authority and the power emanate from God, not man. Whereas we as individuals may be judged for our own lack of sincerity, God does not revoke His own work, *"for God's gifts and his call are irrevocable."*[13] Though the stream may be polluted at various times and places, the fountainhead is pure.

The importance of conveyed blessing from one generation of leadership to another is a biblical principle that dates back as

---

11. 3 John 9-10.
12. 1 Timothy 1:3.
13. Romans 11:29.

far as Isaac and his two sons, Jacob and Esau.[14] The blessing Isaac passed along was, in fact, the *"blessing of Abraham."*[15] Isaac prayed that the blessing he received and passed along to Jacob would also be passed along to Jacob's descendants. When Moses made Aaron the high priest and his two sons priests, he clearly conveyed something of the Lord's blessing when he obeyed God's command: *"After you put these clothes on your brother Aaron and his sons, anoint and ordain them. Consecrate them so they may serve me as priests."*[16] The words *anoint, ordain* and *consecrate* all imply something like the setting apart and blessing that Jacob experienced when his father laid hands upon him and blessed him. The same practice of laying on hands to anoint and bless is found in the setting apart of the Levitical priests: *"You are to bring the Levites before the LORD, and the Israelites are to lay their hands on them."*[17]

The concept of apostolic succession needs to be revisited by the whole church. Whether in unbroken succession or in intermittent succession, there is a continuing and growing need for some type of broadly recognized succession.

The Emerging Leadership Structures of the Primitive Church

The concept of "elders" originates in the Old Testament, but is used in the New Testament as well. The Greek word for "elder" is *presbuteros*. It was used in the Septuagint (the Greek version of the Old Testament, popular at the time of Christ) and later in the New Testament. Its literal meaning is "an older person." The word *presbyter* is a transliteration of *presbuteros* and is often used synonymously with "elder." In the Middle Ages, the word *presbyter* was shortened to *priest*.

---

14. See Genesis 27.
15. Genesis 28:4.
16. Exodus 28:41.
17. Numbers 8:10.

In the Old Testament, families were guided by a patriarch, usually the oldest member or representative of a family, who, along with others in the family who were older and more mature (elders), made decisions for the whole clan. These families grew into tribes that employed the same system. As God established Israel as a nation, this system was used for its government.

At the time of Moses, there were about 3 million Israelites. The system of leadership employed by Moses included the use of elders. Moses acted as the patriarchal authority established by God. He then appointed leaders from those who were recognized elders to help him carry out the work of governing God's people. This would become the pattern for the church.

By the time of the New Testament church, the government of Israel had long since become a monarchy. The synagogues however, still had elders. As the primitive church developed, it did not use what had become the world's system, but reverted back to the earlier pattern of leadership used in the synagogues, along with adapting the pattern Jesus established with the 12 apostles.

When you consider how the early apostles used the Old Testament practice of "casting lots" to replace Judas (as opposed to listening to the voice of the Spirit, as they did later), it is obvious that they were still learning. Later, in response to an unforeseen need, they invented the role of deacons. When Philip made converts outside of Jerusalem, and the Gentile Cornelius was converted with his entire household, the apostles again had to stretch their thinking and appropriately respond. Soon to follow was the institution of elders in far-flung cities. In each case, the apostles were, in fact, experimenting under the delicate guidance of the Holy Spirit since they did not yet have a final version of church structure in place.

The early apostles carried the role of patriarchal authority and then began to appoint elders (presbyters) to assist them in governing an ever-growing church. Local churches began to be formed in distant places very rapidly, which required a new pattern for local church leadership. The apostles could not be physically present at all of the new churches, so they appointed elders to act in their stead and under their authority. We read in Titus 1:5, *"The reason I left you in Crete was that you might straighten out what was left unfinished and appoint elders in every town, as I directed you."* You can see in this verse the passing along of authority from Paul to Titus and then to the elders Titus appointed.

Each local church was governed by a group of elders who remained under the influence of the apostolic authority that had appointed them. This apostolic authority structure remained in place even as the local church developed. An example of this can be found in 1 Corinthians 9:2: *"Even though I may not be an apostle to others, surely I am to you! For you are the seal of my apostleship in the LORD."* When there seemed to be a question of Paul's authority, he reminded the Corinthians that their very existence as a congregation was proof that he was their apostolic authority. He had planted this church and had poured his life into them. They were the "seal," the proof. Even though he was no longer physically present, he retained a position of significant influence as their apostolic authority.

The individuals appointed as elders in the early local churches were clearly not simply administrative leaders, as is often the case today. In fact, the qualifications for elders found in Titus 1:6 and in 1 Timothy 3:1-7 have been used for qualifying ordained ministers (clergy) for two millennia.

This association of elders with the list of qualifications used for ordaining clergy has led many to conclude that elders as described in the New Testament are, in fact, ordained ministers in the apostolic order of ministry. For the most part, this was the universal interpretation until the Reformation.

The Advancement of Apostolic Ministry

The emergence and development of apostolic ministry was an arduous and circuitous process. Though Jesus had clearly commissioned the original 12 apostles, it was not obvious how they were to govern the church as it expanded to different locales.

Imagine how glorious and comfortable it was in the very first church in Jerusalem. The original apostles were there, as were many others who had followed Jesus throughout His earthly ministry. Even His mother and others from His family were there! Peter's first public sermon produced more than three thousand converts, and soon the church had significant public favor.[18] Why should they consider the needs beyond Jerusalem with everything going so well in that city? Though Jesus had commanded them to *"go and make disciples of all nations,"*[19] they seemed content, at first, to remain together where such immediate fruit had begun to manifest. But initial comfort would soon change as persecution began to escalate.

Saul, the great persecutor of the church before his conversion, actually had a hand in its extension. How providential it was that the same man who would one day become the great missionary who so effectively spread the Gospel had a direct hand in the church's growth even while he was trying his best to destroy it. The persecution that Saul provoked caused many believers to leave the spiritual comfort of Jerusalem. They preached everywhere they went.[20] Philip's evangelism outside of Jerusalem also played an important role in this expansion.[21] He did not set all things in order with the newly converted. He preached the Gospel, then moved on to the next place. When the apostles became aware of the conversions and came to visit the newly saved, they began to institute apostolic oversight. *"When the apostles in Jerusalem heard that Samaria had accepted the word of God, they sent Peter and John to them. When they arrived, they prayed for them that they might receive the Holy Spirit, because the Holy Spirit had not yet come upon any of them; they had simply been baptized into the name of the* LORD

---

18. Acts 2:41-47.
19. Matthew 28:19.
20. Acts 8:4.
21. Acts 8:5-13.

Jesus. Then Peter and John placed their hands on them, and they received the Holy Spirit."[22]

Out of this expansion came the need for management of problems in the newly formed churches and the appointing of elders in the different locations where believers began to gather. The apostle Paul was clearly functioning in apostolic authority as he sent his assistant to *"straighten out what was left unfinished and appoint elders in every town, as I directed you."*[23]

The emergence of the church in numerous localities meant that the structure of the Jerusalem church would need development and adjustment. One of the first big tests for the emerging church came over the church's universal stand on the circumcision of Gentiles.

It is entirely impossible to avoid controversy and conflict in the church. From the church's earliest existence, disputes have arisen between good-intentioned brethren. Satan has used this to bring division and diversion from our primary purpose. But God has not left us without biblical examples to deal with conflict, contention or strife over doctrine and church practice. Apostolic governance is an important part of this process.

The entirety of Acts 15 offers a model of apostolic leadership for handling doctrinal controversy. This was the first recorded church council called by those in apostolic authority in the church catholic. The lack of universal recognition of the apostolic role in the church today has left us without the benefit of such apostolic councils for handling doctrinal controversies. But had there been no system of apostolic councils in the early church, we would not have the primary creeds or the canon of Scripture. We would still be plagued by many diabolical controversies like those that challenged the church from its beginning. There is a continuing need for such church councils today. The calling of the church into this type of council has always been complex and a bit messy. Early church fathers

22. Acts 8:14-17.
23. Titus 1:5.

such as Irenaeus, who almost single-handedly held off the intrusion of Gnosticism into the church, and Athanasius, who heroically defended the doctrine of the Trinity, did yeoman service for the church. But these fundamental truths, along with the canonization of Scripture, had to be handled in broadly represented ecumenical church councils. But who would call this type of church council in the present-day church, and who would be called? The lack of broadly recognized apostolic authority makes this needed biblical and historic system of Christian debate difficult to employ.

The issue addressed by the first biblically recorded apostolic church council was primarily doctrinal, although it also modified local church practices. It is interesting to note that the final declaration made by this gathering of leaders was accepted in all the churches everywhere, which demonstrates the council's universally accepted authority.

Verse 6 states: *"The apostles and elders met to consider this question"* of Gentile circumcision. After much discussion, Peter stood and made his comments. Then Barnabas and Paul gave a report of how God was moving among the Gentiles. Afterward, James referred to Peter's comments and then declared his own judgment, which seemed to close the matter. We can learn from this that the system of spiritual leadership was a mixture of consensus leadership and directive leadership. The apostles and elders debated the issues, heard evidence and then came to a general agreement. Clearly, however, there was directive leadership coming from Peter and then James.

The directive leadership that these two influential apostles displayed in this situation has led many theologians to conclude that Peter was a "first among equals" in the universal church (the one holy catholic and apostolic church), and James was a "first among equals" in the Jerusalem church.

Jesus indicated a unique role of leadership for Peter in Matthew 16:18-19: *"'And I tell you that you are Peter, and on this rock I will build my church, and the gates of Hades will not overcome it. I will give you the keys of the kingdom of heaven; whatever you bind on earth will be bound in heaven, and whatever you loose on earth will be loosed in heaven.'"* Later, after Peter's treasonous denial of his association with the Master, Jesus made a special effort to restore Peter to Himself, as well as to his distinctive role in the church.

With regard to James, there are many indications that this brother of Jesus (not the apostle James, brother of John) was indeed the primary leader in the Jerusalem church. Take, for example, Acts 12:17: *"Peter motioned for them to be quiet and described how the Lord had brought him out of prison. 'Tell James and the brothers about this,' he said, and then he left for another place."* Then there is Acts 21:17-19: *"When we arrived at Jerusalem, the brothers received us warmly. The next day Paul and the rest of us went to see James, and all the elders were present. Paul greeted them and reported in detail what God had done among the Gentiles through his ministry."*

In Galatians 1:18-19 and 2:9, we again see Peter highlighted as the principal leader in the church, with James closely associated with both Peter and the Jerusalem church: *"Then after three years, I went up to Jerusalem to get acquainted with Peter and stayed with him fifteen days. I saw none of the other apostles—only James, the Lord's brother." "James, Peter and John, those reputed to be pillars, gave me and Barnabas the right hand of fellowship when they recognized the grace given to me. They agreed that we should go to the Gentiles, and they to the Jews."*

So we see that the oversight roles of the early apostles were clearly recognized beyond the Jerusalem church. We also see that later apostles such as Paul did recognize the unique leadership roles of both James and Peter.

The Emergence of Bishops as Successors to the Apostles

It can be presumed that the primary body of truth that is essential to the church was revealed to and understood by the early apostolic church. The original apostles mentored and discipled many of the early church fathers whose writings were more specific about church structure. We can therefore depend on both the canonized Scriptures and the early writings of the church fathers for contemporary insight.

In the same way that the formation of the canon of Scripture and the primary creeds was a process that required more than three hundred years, the development of the pastoral offices was a process. In the apostolic age, the terms *bishop (episcopoi)* or *presbyter (presbyteroi)* were often used synonymously. By the end of the first century, the office of bishop had developed as separate from the office of presbyter or deacon, and was the successor to the office of apostle. Bishops came to hold the authority to appoint presbyters, as did the early apostles. It was about this same time that the threefold episcopal structure of bishop, presbyter and deacon was universally recognized in the primitive church.

In fact, the office of bishop (as successors to the apostles) actually began to appear while some of the original apostles were still alive. Ignatius of Antioch, who was bishop from about A.D. 67 until he was martyred in A.D. 107, clearly overlaps the time of the New Testament. Only two of the original apostles were dead by the time of Ignatius' consecration as bishop of the very city from which Paul and Barnabas were sent into their traveling apostolic ministry. Clement of Rome, possibly mentioned by Paul as the Clement in Philippians 4:3, became a bishop around A.D. 90. Polycarp, bishop of Smyrna by about A.D. 100, is generally accepted to have been a disciple of the apostle John.

It stands to reason that the living apostles of that time would have attempted to stop the institution of this new office if they had felt it was misguided. But there is evidence that Polycarp was consecrated as a bishop by some of the living apostles and that Ignatius was supported in his office of bishop of Antioch by the apostles. There is certainly no evidence to the contrary.

The bishops soon became the primary form of visible unity in the primitive church. There were no canonized Scriptures during this early period. Thus, it was of highest priority to have proven leaders who had clear authority to teach the words of Christ and carry forth His earthly ministry. While some see the advent of canonized Scripture as the conclusion of the need for bishops as symbols of unity and guardians of the apostolic ministry, most of the church throughout the ages has recognized the continuing need for the ministry of bishops. Even branches of the church that do not recognize the office of bishop look to their ordained clergy to give guidance and oversight to doctrine and apostolic ministry.

Bruce Shelley captures a common concern among evangelicals about the results of this transformation of order in the ancient church when he states: "These changes in the structure and functioning of the church, especially the role of bishops, raise crucial and controversial questions. Christians of nearly every denomination admit that these changes took place. The question is: What do the changes mean and what authority, if any, do they have for the church of later times, especially our own?"[24]

The basis of this question is a legitimate apprehension toward anything that suggests a diminished role for the believer in the life of the church and the fulfillment of its mission. There is logical skepticism toward the episcopal structure, or toward any structure that might take away the responsibility or opportunity for every Christian to fulfill his or her God-given call.

Having been raised in a denomination that emphasizes lay involvement and leadership, I have seen the value and success of involving every Christian in the task. I well remember the almost constant emphasis upon participation in visitation, teaching Sunday school and Training Union, or involvement in other ministries of our local church. Even the constant reference to one another as "brother" or "sister," including the pastor, gave a sense of camaraderie in fulfilling our duty and equality in the ministry.

---

24. Bruce L. Shelley, *Church History in Plain Language*, Word Publishing, Dallas, Texas, 1982, 1985, p. 71.

This type of skepticism caused me to question the contemporary need for "clergy" as defined traditionally. Only after years of biblical study, personal experience as an ordained minister, and a lifetime of helping others fulfill their own personal ministry calls did I inwardly resolve this issue. I came to recognize that the concept of ordained clergy is not an attack on the priesthood of every believer. The two are not mutually exclusive. To the contrary, they are equally important and mutually dependent.

From my denominational background and my subsequent experiences among mostly independent charismatic churches, I have seen both extremes. In many congregations, the spiritual insight and authority of the pastoral ministry is so minimized and dominated by unspiritual or under-qualified laypeople who have administrative power that the churches cannot grow or experience true worship or revival. In other cases, insecure or even unspiritual clergy squelch any true move of God and use their office as a cloak of arrogant separation to deliberately maintain a distance from the laypeople. Thankfully, most churches do not have these extremes, although they may have some level of one or both at work.

Over time, it became obvious to me from scriptural and historical studies, as well as my personal experiences and observations, that God has consistently commissioned the setting apart of those who would serve to lead His people. The right mindset for these formally sanctioned leaders is that they serve as training ministers among ministers in training. They first have the distinct call to be leaders. Then, as they are proven, they are recognized as trainers of others. The wrench in the gear for this biblical system is that many churches and denominations use the Old Testament pattern of the priesthood for their ministers. It was only the Levites who could enter into the Holy Place. It was singularly the high priest who could pass behind the curtain to the Holy of Holies. The majority of the people of God could only stand at a distance and hope for the purity and acceptance before God of those who interceded on their behalf. This kind of pattern for the clergy can lead to confusion of purpose for everyone.

Clarity finally came to me through a statement of a beloved brother, my chief consecrating bishop, the Most Rev. Mike Owen.[25] Archbishop Mike responded to my question about how to balance the role of clergy with the role of every believer as a priest with this simple statement: "The ordained ministry in the lineage of apostolic authority is for the purpose of order, not exclusion."

His answer brought peace to my inner conflict. Yes, the priesthood of every believer must be understood and championed. The members of the ordained presbytery are not an exclusive group who uniquely hold the power to minister; rather, they are coaches and teachers with the distinct purpose of involving all of God's servants in effective ministry. Ephesians 4:11-16 offers a clear pattern of purpose and practice of those in apostolic ministry: "*It was he who gave some to be apostles, some to be prophets, some to be evangelists, and some to be pastors and teachers, to prepare God's people for works of service, so that the body of Christ may be built up until we all reach unity in the faith and in the knowledge of the Son of God and become mature, attaining to the whole measure of the fullness of Christ. Then we will no longer be infants, tossed back and forth by the waves, and blown here and there by every wind of teaching and by the cunning and craftiness of men in their deceitful scheming. Instead, speaking the truth in love, we will in all things grow up into him who is the Head, that is, Christ. From him the whole body, joined and held together by every supporting ligament, grows and builds itself up in love, as each part does its work.*"

The work of all of those engaged in apostolic ministry is to encourage, train and release into effective ministry every gift

---

25. The Most Rev. Mike Owen was the presiding bishop of the Communion of Evangelical Episcopal Churches at the time of my initiation toward consecration as a bishop in 1997. I was consecrated in 1999, with the Most Rev. Wayne Boosahda as my chief consecrator.

within the body of Christ. A church heavily dominated by clergy who mistrust the ability of the whole body to engage in ministry has too often stifled the extension of the kingdom of God in the earth. On the other hand, damage has often been wrought by the overly enthusiastic, under-trained believer who works too independently of the established authority structure.

In the case of the church in the wilderness[26] (the people of Israel), the same God who called the entire nation to be *"'a kingdom of priests and a holy nation'"*[27] also established the Levitical priesthood to coach the people in their role as priests to the nations.[28] This same opportunity exists for the church of today. There is no conflict between the priesthood of every believer and the ordination and recognition of those set apart as clergy. Understanding that the clergy and lay ministry leaders are acting as successors of the apostles is an important element for the full function of all of these leadership roles.

"To him who loves us and has freed us from our sins by his blood, and has made us to be a kingdom and priests to serve his God and Father—to him be glory and power for ever and ever! Amen." Revelation 1:5-6

The Impact of the Reformation on the Pastoral Offices

Thankfully, the concept of "the priesthood of all believers" was recaptured in the Reformation, which began during the sixteenth century. There was a rejection of the belief that all authority to minister and lead the affairs of the church was held exclusively by the ordained clergy. The Reformation created a new class of elders and deacons. Elders and deacons

---

26. Acts 7:38: "'*This is he, that was in the church in the wilderness with the angel which spake to him in the mount Sinai, and with our fathers: who received the lively oracles to give unto us.*'" (KJV)
27. Exodus 19:6.
28. Exodus 28:1-41.

became primarily associated with individual congregations rather than the church universal, and they included those who were not clergy.

The early Presbyterians, for example, recognized that though the ordained clergy carry the responsibility for orthodoxy and the ministry of the sacraments, others who were not so ordained could be equally charged with sharing in the leadership and ministry of the church. They defined the difference in roles by proclaiming the clergy as "teaching elders" and the lay elders as "ruling elders." Some version of this prototype has been adopted by most of the Protestant church.

So, one of the wonderful benefits of the Reformation was to restore lay people back to their needed place in ministry. It also opened the way for the leadership team of the church to have a full range of gifts at work.

In the years preceding the Reformation, the office of bishop had become intermixed with political, economic and military power. Corruption was rampant among many of the bishops throughout Europe. Among an increasing number of both priests and laypeople, spiritual vitality and hunger for genuine Christianity was rising. Timothy George states: "In fact, far from being an age of inane decadence, the two centuries prior to the Reformation proved remarkably vital...while abuses abounded in the Church, so did cries for reform."[29] A division developed between the powerful bishops and reforming priests and monks like Martin Luther and John Calvin. Forerunners of the Reformation such as John Wycliffe and Jan Hus, both of whom were clergy, added to reformational anticlericalism by claiming that not only the bishops but the clergy on all levels were "dens of thieves, nests of serpents, houses of devils."[30]

---

29. Timothy George, *Theology of the Reformers*, Broadman Press, Nashville, 1988, p. 22.

30. E. Gordon Rupp, "Christian Doctrine from 1350 to the Eve of the Reformation," *A History of Christian Doctrine*, Hubert Cunliffe-Jones, ed. (Edinburgh: T. And T. Clark, 1978), p. 292; John Wycliffe, *English Works*, F. D. Matthew, ed. (London: Trubner and Co., 1880), pp. 96-104, 477.

While enormous blessing and the restoration of biblical Christianity came from the Reformation, fierce independence, deficient doctrinal positions and brutal treatment of all who disagreed with the Reformers characterized these times as well. Much of what had been learned, preserved and passed along from one generation to another was lost or forgotten. Perhaps the worst outcome of the Reformation was the deep divisions that came about.

Unfortunately, during the Reformation and throughout the years that have followed, the church has repeatedly divided. It should be noted here that there is general agreement among historians that the intent of the Reformers was to correct the problems in the church of their day, not replace it. While most of the early Reformers recognized the necessity of "valid ministry" through some type of apostolic succession, many of our contemporary expressions of Christ's church have lost the historic and biblical value of the apostolic ministry. Primarily, it is the historic, liturgical/sacramental churches that have maintained apostolic succession. The more evangelical branches of the church have rejected apostolic succession entirely or moved away from its importance, though many have some form of episcopal governance and maintain some system of successive passing of spiritual authority from those who possess it to those who are newly qualified to receive it.

It is a self-evident fact that unity in the "one holy catholic and apostolic church"[31] will not be accomplished by doctrinal debate or symbolic uniformity. God, in His wisdom, gave the primitive church a way for unity to be maintained through the apostolic ministry of bishops. The process of appointment and mutual accountability of those in the apostolic leadership that the primitive church developed helped to bridge the gaps caused by cultural or geographic distance and diverse doctrinal emphases. Since this system of episcopal unity and governance has endured successfully in substantially the same form

---

31. A portion of the Nicene Creed regarding the nature of the church.

since the time of the original apostles, and still continues in many branches of the modern church, we should at least give serious deliberation to the possibility that there is a continuing need and place for the role of apostles/bishops in all streams of the church today.

Key Discussion Points:

1. Apostolic tradition and succession.
2. The advancement of apostolic ministry.
3. The emergence of bishops as successors to the apostles.
4. The impact of the Reformation on pastoral offices.

Questions:

1. Do you see a contemporary need for apostolic authority in the body of Christ?
2. Could you describe how having broadly recognized apostolic authority could benefit the church today?
3. Do you agree with the need to revisit the concept of apostolic succession?

Chapter Six

———— ∞∞∞ ————

Structural Challenges of the Modern Church

The Prophetic and Strategic Leadership Models
———— ∞∞∞ ————

A s we study the church, contemporary or historic, we find certain repeating models that seem to naturally emerge. It is almost as if the church, like the human body, has a DNA that carries within it a genetic code. Whether we intend to or not, certain things always appear as if prompted by some unseen cue from off stage.

What I refer to as the Prophetic and Strategic Leadership Models are examples of genetic code producing what seem, on the surface, to be competing models. In these two seemingly divergent models, we see what could be described as a "parallel paradigm" for spiritual and practical oversight of the people of God. While at times they appear to conflict, they actually are complementary. Many times, those in immediate authority attempt to simply ignore or even destroy the competing model for the sake of an easier operation. But God seems to deny our every effort to produce a leadership model devoid of the tension of these seemingly opposing models.

The Prophetic Leadership Model

From the earliest record of the people of God in the earth, we see a Prophetic Leadership Model that is initiated by God through Adam and carried on by men such as Noah, Abraham, Moses, Jeremiah, Elijah, Elisha and a throng of other prophetic leaders. Most of these prophetic leaders worked miracles, taught Scripture, spoke prophetically and seemed to have little interest in structure. Many were inclined to live separately from the people to whom they ministered and distance themselves from human organization.

In this model, there is a high regard for the person and leading of the Holy Spirit. In other models, an overdependence on systems or human ability can lead to problems, but in this model, there is often a tendency to over-emphasize the ardor of God's presence while ignoring the equally important work of the Holy Spirit to bring order.[1]

Bishop Lesslie Newbigin touched on this important issue: "The preference for the abnormal and the spectacular, the belief that what is extempore and unprepared is more spiritual than what is customary or planned, the tendency to regard order and organization as antithetical to the life of the Spirit— these are all evidences of a conception of the Holy Spirit more characteristic of the Old Testament than the New. In the Old Testament the Holy Spirit is spoken of mainly as a power coming upon individuals at a particular time and enabling them to perform mighty works, to speak God's Word, to discern His will. The New Testament begins by describing how the Holy Spirit descended upon Jesus and abode upon Him, and how in the power of the Spirit He lived and spoke, and how that same Spirit was given to His Church to be the permanent principle

---

1. In Genesis 1:2 we read: *"Now the earth was formless and empty, darkness was over the surface of the deep, and the Spirit of God was hovering over the waters."* Since we know that *"God is not a God of disorder but of peace"* (1 Corinthians 14:33), then we reasonably assume that the Spirit of God was hovering over the chaos in Genesis to assist the process of bringing order.

of its life."[2] Bishop Newbigin's contrast of the tenure of the presence of the Holy Spirit in different human circumstances is critical to understanding how an Old Testament model of the Spirit's attendance is incomplete without a balancing New Testament model. His suggestion of the "abiding" presence of the Holy Spirit explains how humanly managed institutions can be spiritual in nature and provide a legitimate platform for God's guidance and involvement in the earthly church over a long period of time. A "*kairos*"[3] moment of the Holy Spirit's presence or blessing, if it were only temporary, would not abide over an institution created to meet the long-term need, leaving what subsequently occurred lifeless and without anointing.

Take, for instance, the feeding of the poor. We have at least two examples of Jesus feeding the masses that were hungry. So, should we feed the hungry only in a *kairos* moment of super-natural provision, or should we strategically, sacrificially make provision for this important ministry as long as the need exists? Most would agree that we should continue this type of ministry over a long period of time. The point is that, though *kairos* moments are enthusiastically welcomed by all, the abiding presence of the Holy Spirit is also needed. While we cannot hope to have perfect institutions upon the earth, we can trust that God will work within our terrestrial attempts to partner with heaven to fulfill our duties.

Leaders in the prophetic model tend to distrust attempts to institute systems or programs. They are far more dependent upon personal revelation and moment-by-moment leadings from God than on anything that suggests human institution. The obvious benefit of this approach is the high potential for God's imminent blessing and presence. They are beholden to no human system, governmental or religious, and are not

---

2. Lesslie Newbigin, *The Household of God*, Paternoster Press, London, first published 1953 (SCM Press Ltd.), reprinted 1998, pp. 135-136.

3. *Kairos* (Greek): an opportune or seasonable time; the time when things are brought to crisis. It is a moment in which God is fully present; a period in which eternity enters a fixed moment (the time of the Lord).

encumbered by how their utterances might affect others. Their sense of responsibility is to God alone.

But this tendency to disconnect from others has down sides, as well. For instance, what if prophetic leaders are wrong on some point? Those who are convinced that they hear directly from God are difficult to hold accountable. Those who follow an Old Testament model for their prophetic ministry miss the safety and blessing of God's better plan. In the New Testament practice of prophecy, there is accountability. The chief authority of the apostles,[4] combined with the balance of accountability to other proven prophets,[5] brought safety to everyone, especially to the prophet.

Another down side is that while those in the Prophetic Leadership Model can be highly focused upon a specific individual or divine moment, they often cannot express care for the masses or consider the long-term effects of their ministry. Yet we see in God the balanced ability to deal with individuals and the masses, moments in time and eternity, simultaneously.

The Prophetic Model tends to limit leadership to only one person or, at most, a few highly trusted individuals. Moses had to be advised more than once that he could not by himself meet every need of the people entrusted to his oversight.

God clarified to Moses that He was capable of giving to others the same spirit He had given Moses.[6] Even before that, Moses' father-in-law had pointed out that others were competent to join him in his ministry to the people and that the people were suffering as a result of Moses' lack of leadership structure.[7] Many capable leaders fail to recognize that there is a limit to how effective they can be without a Strategic Leadership Model.

The strength of the Prophetic Leadership Model is that it ensures the imminent presence and prophetic Word of God

4. 1 Corinthians 12:28.
5. Galatians 1:19.
6. Numbers 11:10-17.
7. Exodus 18:13-26.

without compromise. Its weakness is its limited accountability and ability to adequately minister to the abundance of diverse needs experienced by the masses over a long period of time.

The Strategic Leadership Model

God instructed Moses to establish a new paradigm of leadership that we will refer to as the Strategic Leadership Model. Aaron was appointed as high priest and his sons as serving priests. This was the beginning of the Levitical priesthood. Though all the people of Israel were to act as priests,[8] God established an order of authority and accountability through the Levitical priesthood. The Levites were empowered by God to maintain a continuity of worship that included the sacrifices, regular reading of Scripture, music and songs, the receiving of offerings, elaborate ceremonies, holy practices, prayer and intercession. Levites helped the poor, settled disputes, and maintained the tabernacle and the later temples. They also became the keepers of the Law of Moses, the Torah, and the subsequent writings of the prophets by acting as the scribes who preserved them in scrolls and the teachers who instructed the people. By the time of Christ's earthly ministry, the spiritual leadership of the Levitical priesthood and the tabernacle worship they oversaw had been extended into a complex system of synagogues, rabbis, Pharisees and Sadducees.

God demonstrated His approval of the model of leadership that He Himself had initiated by granting His miraculous presence and glory. Behold 1 Kings 8:10-11, where we read: *"When the priests withdrew from the Holy Place, the cloud filled the temple of the LORD. And the priests could not perform their service because of the cloud, for the glory of the LORD filled his temple."* In the middle of their plan, God intervened. Since God establishes order, it neither offends nor limits Him. If the established order does not welcome Him, He simply overwhelms it or bypasses it altogether.

---

8. Exodus 19:6.

The obvious weaknesses of a Strategic Leadership Model include overdependence on form, lack of sensitivity to God and others, exclusiveness and arrogance, and the ability to maintain and extend itself without the manifest presence of God. Leaders from the Strategic Model often become overly dependent upon systems, programs and past performance. Preservation of what has been and dutiful continuation of the same can become their primary pursuits. Leadership systems without the Spirit are dangerous: *"These are the men who divide you, who follow mere natural instincts and do not have the Spirit."*[9] A more subtle but equally insidious effect of overdependence on the Strategic Leadership Model is that it ignores or slowly bleeds away an individual's uniqueness and innovativeness. Because of reliance on the system and proven methods, healthy individuality can be stifled or even suppressed. This is contrary to the fact that God created each of us with purpose and destiny, which must be encouraged, nurtured and released into effective ministry.

These two paradigms, the Prophetic Leadership Model and the Strategic Leadership Model, give us a basis for understanding how God continues to bring leadership to His church today. As in the past, we need to have the true presence of God's power and voice, combined with a system of accountability that provides historical continuity along with strategic extension of the church. God has allowed a tension and balance to develop between these two distinct but inseparable models.

It seems that on many levels God has designed us to live in holy tension between two seemingly competing truths. Salvation, for instance, is granted by grace through faith and cannot be earned through human works.[10] Yet faith requires works to be genuine.[11] So works and faith complement one

---

9. Jude 19.
10. Ephesians 2:8-9.
11. James 2:14-24.

another and are both necessary for salvation. A saving faith that cannot be earned through works is dead without works. This is holy tension. The Word and the Spirit, another distinct but inseparable tandem, work together to bring out the full texture of truth.

Dr. David Shibley comments: "Tension is not necessarily a bad word. It is possible—indeed, it is necessary in our day—to live in the reality of many healthy tensions. Much of the strength of our Christian faith is derived from apparent paradoxes. In fact, they are healthy tensions. For instance, there is the strong, healthy paradox of the sovereignty of God and the free will of humanity. Both doctrines are immutably true. Yet the strength of each is derived from the veracity of the other."[12]

So it seems that God has designed the Prophetic Leadership Model and the Strategic Leadership Model to provide a balance; a holy tension of prophetic (Spirit-led) leadership and strategic (Word-led) leadership. Why should there be a conflict between order and the move of the Spirit? The key here is dependence upon the Word and the Spirit in each model. Though each model may lean toward one primary form of God's leadership, leaders in each model can learn to be led by both the Word and Spirit. There must be mutual respect and cooperation between the two models to achieve God's designed balance.

Of course, these models can present problems when we attempt to make them work within the context of modern laws and expectations.

The Modern Church

As already stated, one of the wonderful benefits of the Reformation was to restore laypeople to their rightful place

---

12. David Shibley, *A Force in the Earth*, Creation House, Orlando, Florida, 1989, 1997, p. 111.

alongside the apostles, prophets, evangelists, pastors and teachers in ministry. It also opened the way for the leadership team of the church to have a full range of gifts at work. 1 Corinthians 12:27-28 states: *"Now you are the body of Christ, and each one of you is a part of it. And in the church God has appointed first of all apostles, second prophets, third teachers, then workers of miracles, also those having gifts of healing, those able to help others, those with gifts of administration, and those speaking in different kinds of tongues."*

In this listing we find *"those with gifts of administration"* listed along with those having the more ministry-oriented gifts. However, the need for giftings of administration, coupled with the legal requirement for an administrative group to act as a board of directors for a nonprofit corporation, has led to new conflicts. The biblical mandate is that elders are to be spiritual leaders, not simply administrative leaders who legally supervise a nonprofit corporation. The law and, for that matter, the general public require that a nonprofit corporation have qualified directors who have sufficient business acumen to protect the solvency and mission of the corporation. These two incongruous requirements put increasingly strenuous demands upon church leadership.

The historical patterns for church government are difficult to use today because culture has changed in the modern world. The management of local churches is very different today than it was two millennia ago, four centuries ago, one century ago or even 30 years ago.

Initially, the church was *"all together in one place."*[13] Unity and ministry to everyone was relatively natural and flowed out of their shared *"koinonia."* *"They devoted themselves to the apostles' teaching and to the fellowship, to the breaking of bread and to prayer. Everyone was filled with awe, and many wonders and miraculous signs were done by the apostles. All the believers were together and had everything in common. Selling*

---

13. Acts 2:1.

their possessions and goods, they gave to anyone as he had need. Every day they continued to meet together in the temple courts. They broke bread in their homes and ate together with glad and sincere hearts, praising God and enjoying the favor of all the people. And the Lord added to their number daily those who were being saved."[14] What a dynamic local church! This church in Jerusalem can best be described as more of a "community of faith" than a congregation. Yes, problems did emerge, but the church had respected and proven leadership combined with corporate enthusiasm. They found simple solutions, made easy adjustments and rolled forward until persecution broke out against them.

Fast forward to the church of one hundred years ago. Local churches were mostly rural, small and simple to manage. People who attended a church lived within walking distance or, at most, a horseback or buggy ride away. Usually, entire families attended the same church and took care of one another's needs since they were in close proximity to one another. Families would generally stay in the same area and the same church their entire lives. Grandparents, aunts and uncles, cousins, nephews and nieces—they were all there. Even in the large cities, neighborhoods were stable; and many of the emotional and spiritual needs were handled by people who lived, worshiped, worked and played together for a lifetime.

Since biblical times, only the cathedrals and primary denominational churches of the great cities had been large and diverse in ministries and staff. A church with an attendance of one thousand was almost unheard of until this century. Many churches had no regular clergy since the majority of congregations were dependent upon circuit preachers. Only the largest churches in America had a professional church staff, much less multiple ordained ministers.

The invention of modern transportation, especially the automobile, changed the nature of churches forever. Since

---

14. Acts 2:42-47.

World War II, churches have been dramatically transformed, especially in the major urban areas around the world. For instance, most churches in America are now located in or near a city. As the general population gravitated to urban areas and became more mobile, the nature of local churches changed as well. In our modern, mobile society, people move from one church to another frequently. Denominational identification and doctrinal issues are less important to the average Christian today. Instead, they are more likely to choose a church home for reasons of convenience, style, personal preferences or relationships with members. Churches are larger on average, and the expectation level of their congregants has risen sharply. Small churches labor under constant comparison to the very largest and most successful churches in America, especially those that are televised and watched by congregants getting dressed to go to a service. Words, specialized terms and phrases have sprung up from this phenomenon of change, such as *megachurch, metachurch, youth minister* and *children's pastor, church-hopping, church-growth principles, church software, counselor's liability insurance, keeping the back door closed, church marketing* and *seeker-sensitive.*

Local churches are now expected to be as efficient as IBM and concurrently as warm, caring and friendly as your favorite grandmother's kitchen. They must have great music, world-class ministry programs, clean facilities with well-manicured landscaping, sufficient and well-lighted parking, video graphics, technology and the proper temperature.

A successful pastor can no longer be an average pulpiteer and caregiver. He or she must now have extensive educational degrees, be a competent counselor in a broad variety of psychological and spiritual disciplines, be proficient in recruiting and managing a staff as well as managing a business, be competent in developing a wide range of divergent ministries simultaneously, be accountable for continual church growth and be current on social and spiritual issues. A pastor must be prophetic, prayerful, apostolic and sociable, and do all this with a Christ-like attitude and an attentive ear to the regular counsel, suggestions and advice of denominational leaders, a library of books, magazine articles, conferences, a church board, a staff and a congregation.

A church board now must deal with an operation that has multiple ministers and staff people, plus high demands and expectations from the congregation and community (including many of the same demands with which an ordained minister must deal). Board members must comply with high expectations, being especially wise, responsible, committed and, above all, spiritual. Commonly, they must also help oversee or manage a corporation with a multimillion-dollar debt, facility and yearly budget. Governmental regulations and legal liability issues are other responsibilities with which a church board must grapple.

Tension often develops between the church board and the pastoral staff over roles, responsibilities and lines of authority. Many of these conflicts arise when ministers do not have sufficient training or experience to deal with administrative issues, or board members do not have sufficient training or experience to deal with ministry, program or doctrinal issues. Pastor Ted Haggard weighs in on this important issue as he states: "All modern churches have two structures within them. One is the spiritual body, the other the corporation. Jesus Christ is the head of the spiritual body with pastors who teach, elders who support, deacons who serve, apostles who lead, evangelists who win the lost, and overseers and bishops who bless and protect. The Bible is their guide and the Holy Spirit provides the life for this living organism, the true Church."[15] He further comments: "If the spiritual body wants to use their tithes to finance missions, own a building, or hire people to coordinate meetings, then the spiritual body must form a corporation to perform these functions. Corporations perform practical functions that do cost money. They have officers, boards and members that

---

15. Ted Haggard, *The Life Giving Church*, Regal Books, Ventura, California, 1998, p. 113.

govern them. Corporations own assets, incur liabilities, employ personnel and set budgets. Many churches effectively use their corporations to further the ministry of the church. Too often, however, as years pass, the corporation slowly starts to dominate the spiritual Body. Once this happens, the spiritual Body becomes the servant of the corporation and the purpose of believers' meetings becomes the receiving of offerings, the selling of religious products and increasing assets." Frequently, these problems emanate from a lack of mutual understanding and respect, yet some of the problems stem from the use of old paradigms for modern circumstances.

In the New Testament, we see an underground, illegal band of churches that has no concerns with regard to a church board held accountable by a state or federal government. Even at the time of the Reformation, legal issues of church government initially were not a concern. Like the primitive churches, early protestant congregations were illegal and generally persecuted. Those that were not illegal usually became a direct arm of the secular government, such as the Lutherans in Germany and the Anglicans in England.

The issues we deal with today are new and require fresh paradigms. How do we balance the need for pastors to truly lead from an apostolic and prophetic capacity, give place to the priesthood of all believers through active leadership on the level of elders, and meet the legal and administrative requirements of a modern church? These are the questions with which contemporary church leaders must wrestle.

We have already looked at 1 Corinthians 12:27-28 as a biblical example of specific ministry gifts needed by the church. And in this same passage we can see an actual line of authority put forth by God: *"Now you are the body of Christ, and each one of you is a part of it. And in the church God has appointed first of all apostles, second prophets, third teachers, then workers of miracles, also those having gifts of healing, those able to help others, those with gifts of administration, and those speaking in different kinds of tongues."* The authority flows from the apostles to the other ministry-oriented giftings, then to the administrative level, then to the local expression of worship. Notice again the order: apostles, those in apostolic ministry, helps and administration, then worship and outreach.[16]

In Acts 6, we see a model for handling administrative problems. In verses 1-4 we read: *"In those days when the number of disciples was increasing, the Grecian Jews among them complained against those of the Aramaic-speaking community because their widows were being overlooked in the daily distribution of food. So the Twelve gathered all the disciples together and said, 'It would not be right for us to neglect the ministry of the word of God in order to wait on tables. Brothers, choose seven men from among you who are known to be full of the Spirit and wisdom. We will turn this responsibility over to them and will give our attention to prayer and the ministry of the word.'"*

The office of deacon was established to help superintend the ministry to those in need. Over time, the role of deacons included many other administrative responsibilities. But by the Reformation, the role of deacon began to be confused with the historical role of elder. This confusion often persists even today. In the sacramental branches of the church, the office of deacon is considered the first step toward priesthood (becoming a presbyter). Deacons are ordained as clergy and can fulfill most of the duties of a presbyter with the exception of performing the sacraments. In the evangelical branches, the deacon can represent anything from a "glorified usher" to something more akin to an elder. In the latter case, deacons are often more influential and have more authority over all local church matters, spiritual and administrative, than the pastors. These deacons as described here are generally laypeople who, while being fully capable as dedicated participants in ministry, generally do not rise to the level of calling or qualification to

---

16. The identification of "speaking in different kinds of tongues" as a worship and outreach function is speculative, but is based upon its use in 1 Corinthians 14 as both an instrument of blessing to the believers and as a "sign" to the unbelievers.

be clergy in the universal church. This system often removes the unique roles of the clergy, who represent historic and biblical apostolic authority.

Again, let me emphasize that there are two very different views in the church regarding deacons. One view is the long-standing, historic view that deacons are apostolically linked to bishops and presbyters as a functional part of the episcopate. In this view, they are clergy, having met similar requirements to those who are called to vocational ministry as clergy, and by virtue of their training and apostolic ordination, are to be recognized by the church universal and to minister in it.

The other prevailing view is that which was commonly embraced during and after the Reformation by a broad spectrum of evangelical Protestant churches. This view holds that a deacon is more of a local church-based person, generally a layperson who has the call to faithful service to God and who, having been proven in the local congregation as having met biblical requirements for the deaconate, is ordained to that role. In this case, the role of the deacon is primarily fulfilled within the local congregation and is not considered to be a call to vocational ministry as a clergy person.

There is a valid need for both views and, though it may seem difficult to understand how they can coincide, the benefits of making this twofold view of the deaconate (universal church clergy/deacons as opposed to local church laity/deacons) functional will be worthwhile.

Three Centers of Local Church Leadership

From my study of the passages of Scripture we have mentioned, and from my own experience, I conclude that there are three primary centers of authority that must work in tandem for a healthy local church.

First, there is the apostolic authority. This authority flows from the episcopate (bishops, presbyters and deacons). This is often referred to as the fivefold ministry, found in

Ephesians 4:11-12: "*It was he who gave some to be apostles, some to be prophets, some to be evangelists, and some to be pastors and teachers, to prepare God's people for works of service, so that the body of Christ may be built up.*" These are the apostolically ordained presbyters (clergy) who have been qualified to oversee the ministry of the Word and sacraments. They are a part of and therefore under the direct spiritual authority of the episcopate. They do not select themselves, but are ordained by others who have apostolic authority. Their ordination represents a "setting apart" into the universal church as ministers. For this reason, education, mentorship and levels of apprenticeship are typically associated with this level of ordination.

Second, there is the local team of elders or "presbyters" that assures the diversity of ministry to the local church. The ordained clergy presbyters appoint and serve alongside lay elders or "lay presbyters," who, while not being clergy, are qualified to bring spiritual leadership to the local congregation. The lay elders should also meet the biblical requirements for this position, but do not normally require the extensive education and apprenticeship since their ordination is only for their own local church and not for the universal church.

Third, there is the administrative authority (church board, vestry, deacon board, etc.) that supervises the administrative and legal work of the church. This is a legal church board consisting of qualified individuals from the congregation who are selected by some agreed-upon system of election that is consistent with current secular law.

Beyond these primary centers of authority and leadership, there are other vital leadership areas, such as the ministry staff, the church staff, department and specialty ministry leaders, care-group leaders, Christian education leaders and the list goes on, based upon the extent of organized ministry at work in the individual local church.

As the anointing oil flowed from the top of the High Priest Aaron's head, over his beard and down his collar, so anointing will flow into our congregations as we get our leaders into proper position and function.

The challenge before us is to develop a pattern for local church structure that is biblically and historically sound. It must be a structure that is faithful to its apostolic nature, yet addresses the unique administrative and legal requirements of the contemporary church. There must be a balance of authority and leadership that reflects the various leadership giftings within the local congregation. A viable connection from the local church to the church universal and a reciprocal connection from the church translocal to the church local should be in place. What will future local church leadership structure look like and how will it relate to the universal church? It is precisely this question that we now deliberate.

We must allow Ephesians 4:11-16 to serve as both a guide for our structure and the ultimate goal for what we are doing: "*It was he who gave some to be apostles, some to be prophets, some to be evangelists, and some to be pastors and teachers, to prepare God's people for works of service, so that the body of Christ may be built up until we all reach unity in the faith and in the knowledge of the Son of God and become mature, attaining to the whole measure of the fullness of Christ. Then we will no longer be infants, tossed back and forth by the waves, and blown here and there by every wind of teaching and by the cunning and craftiness of men in their deceitful scheming. Instead, speaking the truth in love, we will in all things grow up into him who is the Head, that is, Christ. From him the whole body, joined and held together by every supporting ligament, grows and builds itself up in love, as each part does its work.*" Our church structures must allow all giftings to fully function so that each member may grow into the fullness of God's destiny for them. Leaders will function in their divine giftings and every need will be met. The result will be that we will all grow in God's love and maturity, and corporately fulfill His will.

Key Discussion Points:

1. The Prophetic Leadership Model.
2. The Strategic Leadership Model.

3. The modern church.
4. Three centers of local church leadership.

Questions:

1. Have you experienced either positive or negative effects of the tension between the Prophetic and the Strategic Leadership Models?
2. Beyond those described by the author, can you think of other ways the modern church differs from the church of one hundred years ago?
3. Do you agree that there is a need for fresh paradigms in ministry today?
4. What special structural needs could the future hold for the church?

Chapter Seven

———∝∝∝———

Future Church

What will the church universal and apostolic look like in the future? As the prayer of Jesus that we will be one and the command of Jesus that we go into all the world are fulfilled, the church will become the *"radiant church"*[1] about which the apostle Paul prophetically spoke. Our obedience to His command and the unifying work of the Holy Spirit will combine to give us a thorough washing, the outcome being a church that will shine with irresistible brilliance, even to the darkest corners of the earth. Our spirit-empowered catholicity and apostolicity will lead us into a glorious future and the return of our Lord and Savior, Jesus Christ.

We have devoted most of the emphasis of this book to the unity of the church to this point. Now let us turn toward its apostolicity.

---

1. Ephesians 5:27.

The Restoration of the Truly Apostolic Church

From the early days of the modern Pentecostal movement, there was much discussion about the restoration of the apostolic ministry. Charles F. Parham, one of the movement's leaders, referred to the "apostolic faith," and this description of the movement became broadly utilized. From its introduction at the beginning of the twentieth century, modern Pentecostalism emphasized the works and teachings of the early apostles and promoted the revival of apostolic ministry in the churches. But while the apostolic tradition was emphasized by the apostolic faith movement, the office or authority of the apostle in the apostolic succession was not.

There is a resurging interest in the role of apostles and bishops among many segments of the evangelical church today. Many have concluded that the historical episcopate has much to offer. I, too, have a profound respect for the episcopal system of church government. Years of experience in church planting and translocal ministry have taught me the value of accountability, oversight, synergism and encouragement that comes from being a functional part of a leadership team.

My Baptist upbringing and my years of involvement in the charismatic stream of the church have encouraged independence and autonomy. This tendency toward self-governing individualism has been a point of inward conflict for me. I have been involved with a multitude of problems that arise when there is little or no accountability for pastors or missionaries beyond their own church boards, and when local churches have no translocal infrastructures or authorities upon which they can depend in times of difficulty. The attitude of self-reliance that is so prevalent in many segments of the church goes against what I see in Scripture and has been repeatedly discredited in my own ministry experiences.

In his book *The New Apostolic Churches*,[2] Dr. C. Peter
Wagner points out that there is a growing trend toward what
he calls "the New Apostolic Reformation." He goes on to outline some of the common characteristics of the new "apostolic
network churches" being formed around the world.

For many years I have closely observed various attempts,
both successful and unsuccessful, to form new networks or fellowships of churches and ministers, especially among independent charismatic churches and ministries. Most of these
fellowships have purposely distanced themselves from anything
that would make them appear like denominational structures,
although some, by their own admission, are indeed denominations. They are typically very low-key in their organizational
framework and, in most cases, lack any real authority over their
member ministers or local churches other than relational influence. There is a wide range of practices among these fellowship
networks, from those that are strictly a "fellowship," primarily
gathering for the purpose of association, friendship and frater-
nity, to those that view themselves as "apostolic networks," with
tighter rules, expectations and accountability.

One of the strongest points among these emerging apostolic
structures is, in fact, their emphatic emphasis upon relationships
over organizational structures. Church structures, all too often,
become far more administrative than relational. While relation-
ship-based structures are complicated, and can be difficult to
establish and maintain over great distances or over a long period
of time, they more fully mirror the biblical approach to leadership. The test seems to be time. The longer the tenure of these
networks, the greater the tendency to drift into primarily organizational structures, repeating the very problem of being overly
administrative, as opposed to primarily relational, that is so
common in traditional denominations. An overly administrative
approach is, of course, the very characteristic they want to avoid.

---

2. C. Peter Wagner, *The New Apostolic Churches*, Regal Books, Ventura,
California, 1998 p. 14.

However, I have noted dissatisfaction and disappointment among both the leaders and members of some of these fellowships and networks. Some are retracing their steps and are thoughtfully studying history to find relevant structures for today. Others are joining existing denominations that they once may have scorned. Perhaps this trend is a work of the Holy Spirit to position us for higher cooperation and effectiveness. It may also represent a convergence of the ancient and the contemporary traditions and streams.

The comments of the apostolic leaders interviewed in Dr. Wagner's book indicate that their view of the contemporary office of the apostle is varied, but they clearly recognize that there is a continuing role for apostolic ministry. Their position on historic apostolic succession in the traditional sense is not at all clear from the limited reports from Dr. Wagner's book, which, of course, was not intended to be an exhaustive analysis of these apostolic networks. On the surface, there is virtually no indication of an embrace of a historic view of apostolic ministry among these newly emerging apostolic leaders. We get only a superficial knowledge of their views and how they came to hold them, so I admit that there may be a much deeper understanding and evaluation of historic apostolicity on the part of any or all of the apostolic network leaders described. While these movements surely would benefit from such considerations, they should be commended for their intent to verify their structures and practices biblically, a point often lost in the historic church. I know some of these network movements firsthand, and I must say that there is much to be admired and considered from their successes.

An absence of universally accepted standards of orthodoxy and behavior lessens the impact of the apostolic ministry. Such standards will eventually be needed, even in those networks that are intentionally loosely organized. It seems there remains room for much growth and understanding. John Kelly, one of the pioneer leaders in the development of modern apostolic networks, alludes to this need for further development of understanding among these emerging apostles when he states,

"The apostolic movement is no longer in the formulation phase; it is currently going through a maturation process."[3] In this maturation process, my hope is that these emerging leaders will consider all of the available resources, which include the time-proven lessons that can be learned from a study of the two thousand year history of apostolic practice.

In Genesis 26:18-19, we see a biblical blueprint for contemporary leaders as we attempt to implement change in the modern church: "*Isaac reopened the wells that had been dug in the time of his father Abraham, which the Philistines had stopped up after Abraham died, and he gave them the same names his father had given them. Isaac's servants dug in the valley and discovered a well of fresh water there.*" From this passage we discover the benefit of using what our "fathers" dug up, even while we continue the effort to find something new and fresh. We see the children of Israel standing on the shoulders of those who had gone before them and adding to those inherited blessings by digging new wells. Our fathers from every age of church history offer important lessons of understanding for us. Both their successes and failures have contemporary value. It is part of God's design that we walk in blessings that we did not create or deserve, but which, are passed along to us: "*And it shall be, when the LORD thy God shall have brought thee into the land which he sware unto thy fathers, to Abraham, to Isaac, and to Jacob, to give thee great and goodly cities, which thou buildedst not, and houses full of all good things, which thou filledst not, and wells digged, which thou diggedst not, vineyards and olive trees, which thou plantedst not....*"[4] In this case, Israel inherited blessings that actually came from the heathen. Lessons and blessings from every source become a pathway to increased effectiveness for those who learn from them.

---

3. C. Peter Wagner, *The New Apostolic Churches*, Regal Books, Ventura, California, 1998, p. 42. John Kelly is the overseeing apostle of Antioch Churches and Ministries.
4. Deuteronomy 6:10-11 (KJV).

Along these same lines, we read in Deuteronomy 19:14, *"Do not move your neighbor's boundary stone set up by your predecessors in the inheritance you receive in the land the LORD your God is giving you to possess."* The warning to us in the church of today is to use great care in moving inherited boundaries. The ancient creeds, the canon of Scripture, the apostolic ministry and many other "boundaries" were set in place long ago by our spiritual predecessors. While we engage in possessing spiritual, doctrinal and strategic territory that God gives us in this generation, we must take care to not ignore that which has gone before us. Like Abel's blood crying out from the ground, our predecessors' blood has a voice that we must heed. As God brings the contemporary church into "new territory," we should gratefully and willingly receive those things that God allows to be passed to us from those who previously walked this ground.

An unfortunate habit that is far too common is to think of the modern church as a more "authentic" example of the church. In this way of thinking, most of the church's history is shrouded in spiritual darkness and, therefore, there is no need for continuity with it. Yet the same people who discount the writings of the early church fathers and practically everything else from the historical traditions confidently believe that those same early church leaders were guided by the Holy Spirit as they canonized Scripture or established the primary historical creeds. Perhaps our discriminating view of the primitive church needs to be reconsidered. This is especially true for those who have strong opinions about the irrelevancy of the historical church and its practices despite never having seriously studied the issues or the writings of the early church fathers.

A proper understanding of the church requires relating to the ancient, universal Christian church and maintaining continuity with it. It is easy to claim to do this. A local church in the evangelical tradition boldly declares on its sign, "Founded A.D. 33." But does this proclamation, no matter how sincere, make it so? It does not follow logic that a church can claim a historic and uninterrupted connection with a church that it believes has been apostate during much of its history.

In the Old Testament, David recognized the granted authority of King Saul, even as Saul was intent upon killing him. Saul had discredited himself with God by his own evil behavior, but he still was the king of Israel. When David had Saul in a place where he could have killed him, he did not. He cut off a corner of King Saul's robe in a cave, but was later *"conscience-stricken"*[5] for having done it. He then did everything in his power to restore his relationship with God's ordained authority. Saul himself testified that because of David's behavior that day in the cave, David would be king after Saul's death. David honored the office even while Saul behaved in an ungodly manner. Because of his honorable conduct, David later received blessing from God. Ultimately, Saul was killed and David ascended to the throne. Though Saul was judged by God for his failures, the office he held was passed on to David in an order of succession that God Himself preserved. Keep in mind that David was *anointed* by God to be the king of Israel long before he received *permission* from God to walk in that office. While the anointing is critical to any office to which God calls us, it is just as critical to *receive* that office according to God's divine order.

In the same way that God preserved the anointing and consecration of the office for David through the years of ungodly actions by King Saul, the succession of authority in the church is not directly damaged by the failures of those who have received it or passed it along. God has preserved the pastoral offices even through the darkest times of the church's history. A false prophet cannot destroy prophecy, a false teacher cannot destroy truth and a false apostle cannot destroy the office of apostle.

God has commanded us to respect humanly instituted authorities. In 1 Peter 2:13 we read, *"Submit yourselves for the*

---

5. 1 Samuel 24:5.

Lord's sake to every authority instituted among men." We are later told to *"Show proper respect to everyone"* and to *"honor the king."*[6] The apostle Paul admitted his mistake when he did not give proper respect to the high priest, calling him a *"white-washed wall"* and a *lawbreaker.*[7] Even though this high priest seemed to deserve the insults, Paul realized that he would be held accountable before God for his disrespect for an office that God had established.

The history of the church is filled with strong words, often inappropriately spoken against those in authority. We must be careful with our actions and words toward those who have gone before us in these offices that God Himself has ordained, especially in the pastoral offices that carry forth and pass along the apostolicity of the church from generation to generation. Due care must be given to treating the offices established in the church with honor and respect.

We must be clear, however, that the pastoral offices are not positions of honor, but rather, of service. In reference to the office of bishop, St. Augustine of Hippo stated: "A 'bishop' who has set his heart on a position of eminence rather than an opportunity for service should realize that he is no bishop."[8] A.B. Bruce, commenting on the original 12 apostles upon whom the office of bishop is modeled, stated, "Those on whom so much depended, it plainly behooved to possess very extraordinary qualifications. The mirrors must be finely polished that are designed to reflect the image of Christ."[9]

Christ Himself trained and proved the quality of character of those He appointed. Still, they were by no means perfect. Sufficient time should be given to the education and formation of those appointed to the office of bishop under the careful oversight of those already proven.

---

6. 1 Peter 2:17.
7. Acts 23:3-5.
8. Augustine of Hippo, *City of God*, 19:19.
9. A. B. Bruce, *The Training of the Twelve*, Kregel Publications, Grand Rapids, Michigan, 1971, p. 13. Reproduced from the Fourth Edition, Revised and Improved, 1894 by A.C. Armstrong and Son.

The great missionary statesman J. Oswald Sanders suggested that the office of bishop is of little value if there is no proven, godly character: "It should be observed that it is not the office of overseer but the function of overseeing that Paul asserts is honorable and noble. It is the most privileged work in the world, and its glorious character should be an incentive to covet it because, when sought from highest motives, it yields both present and eternal dividends. In Paul's mind, only deep love for Christ and genuine concern for His church would provide men with sufficiently powerful motive to aspire to that office. But in most lands today Christian leadership confers prestige and privilege; and unworthy ambition may easily induce self-seeking and unspiritual men to seek the office."[10] Any position of Christian leadership should be sought only in God's way and for His purposes. All other motives and all other paths are doomed to failure.

I have noticed of late that many are proclaiming themselves to be apostles or bishops. The appointment of oneself to the office of bishop is without scriptural merit and is fundamentally in opposition to the point of being one in the first place. If there is no validation by other bishops, no accountability to orthodoxy and no proven signs, then there is no basis for a person to hold that office. What credibility is there when spiritual authority is self-proclaimed? Can a person be a symbol of unity while insisting on autonomy?

The absence of generally recognized standards for those in apostolic ministry among independent churches has encouraged this tendency to self-appoint. I am quite sure that many have sincerely tried to obey their call from God in seeking this office. They did not intend to self-appoint, but knowing no other method, they merely adopted what seemed the only solution. But the outcome of this method is that their apostleship or bishopric will be continually questioned by those who

---

10. John Oswald Sanders, *Spiritual Leadership*, 1902, published by Moody Press, Chicago, 1967, 1980, pp. 18-19.

have followed a more traditional path through a qualified succession to their appointment.

Consider this proclamation from the 1958 gathering of Anglican bishops: "Ordination must be performed by those who have received and are acknowledged to have received, authority to exercise episcope in the Body, and to admit others to share in that ministry. This acknowledgement by the Body of the ministry of episcope must be recognized and accepted. From this arises the principle of continuity by succession, which appears to be indispensable, at least from a human standpoint."[11] Those who have carefully preserved the apostolic succession have a vested interest in the lineage of those who now claim this office, since the very idea of succession is that it does not originate with the one who claims it. While it is probable that those to whom this issue matters most may find it difficult to see beyond the past into the future, beyond what has been into what will be, we must still consider their knowledge and historical position on the practice of and succession of this office. The past is not always the best road map for the future, but the weight of hundreds of years of experience must at least be seriously examined.

There is a growing need for a widely recognized system for appointing bishops and, for that matter, all who claim the role of clergy in the modern church, especially among the evangelical, non-liturgical branches. The traditional system, practiced among the liturgical churches that recognize apostolic succession, is a time-honored and biblically based method. It has flaws and potential for abuse, but still may provide the best model for the restoration of this important office. Those who have practiced these things historically have made certain conclusions that are worthy of our consideration.

An agreed-upon definition of the office of bishop would help. Some would argue that any pastor or Christian leader who has an extended jurisdiction of oversight beyond a

---

11. 1958 Lambeth Conference of Anglican bishops.

medium-sized congregation is in fact functioning in a form of bishopric. The pastor of a megachurch or larger is often in administrative and spiritual oversight of many clergy and usually has some network connection and spiritual oversight of at least a few other outside churches and pastors. Would this constitute a bishopric? Is the leader of a parachurch ministry (international, regional or otherwise) that plants churches or other ministries that continue to relate back to him a bishop? Should a district overseer, area supervisor, association president, network leader or any number of other titled individuals be considered bishops? In other words, can we find terminology and insights that will help us redefine how we relate to one another across traditionally un-crossable lines?

The above questions, along with many others, must be addressed, but address them we must.

In his book *Spheres of Authority*,[12] Dr. C. Peter Wagner raises many interesting and potentially controversial points about the office of apostle, applying a whole new depictive nomenclature to that office. Wagner's liberal use of the title "apostle" to individuals who represent a variety of specialized ministries and jurisdictions is worthy of further deliberation. Wagner's insights, when combined with Dr. Donald MacGavran's[13] studies and conclusions on unreached people groups, offer fresh insight into how jurisdictions could be redefined in the modern church.

The jurisdiction of bishops has historically been tied to geographic territories. The New Testament apostles did seem to function territorially, but not purely geographically. The apostle Paul's ministry was intentionally conducted in territories beyond those already reached. There was, however, the predictable "crossing over" that occurred because of his specific call to the Gentiles. There is also the issue of more than

---

12. C. Peter Wagner, *Spheres of Authority*, Wagner Publications, 2002.
13. Donald MacGavran, author of *Bridges of God*, was a third-generation missionary to India who is considered by many as the father of the modern church-growth movement.

one apostle ministering among a particular church or group of churches. In this case, Paul defended his apostolic rights of oversight on the basis of his unique relationship with these churches as their founder and father in the faith.

These issues lead to a need for reexamining the historical concept of territorial jurisdiction based *solely* on geography. Most of the modern apostolic networks, even those with a decidedly sacramental/historical bent are using non-geographical jurisdictions that are relationally or ethnically based. The Orthodox branches of the church have used ethnically based jurisdictions for most of their history. They have a combined territorial/ethnic-based jurisdiction. This adds even more texture to this needed discussion.

Wagner's efforts to understand modern apostolic ministry and its importance and functions should challenge us to reexamine our notions about this office of ministry. Even a dialogue of disagreements would be preferable to ignoring this vital subject altogether.

The current needs of the church worldwide and our common commission to take the Gospel to every tribe, people and nation combine to demand true grassroots reformation. Therefore, there should be a system by which bishops are accountable to biblical apostolicity, historic apostolicity and contemporary counterpart bishops. Developing this process will be difficult, but it promises greater understanding and cooperation for Christians on every level.

Perhaps the greatest challenge for any of us is to recognize that the path that has guided us to our current structures includes a mixture of biblical principles, historical patterns and more recent cultural traditions. In commenting on this issue, Van Engen asserted: "In practice, most Protestant groups formed traditions nearly as binding as the [Roman] Catholics and established similar sets of authorities: ecumenical councils, confessional creeds, synodical legislation, church orders, and theologians (especially founders) of a particular church. Those free churches, particularly in America, that claim to stand on Scripture alone and to recognize no traditional authorities are in some sense least free because they are not even conscious of what traditions have molded their understanding of Scripture."[14] The first step forward is to openly examine ourselves, and with as little prejudgment as possible, to reexamine the potential legitimacy and efficacy of other historical and contemporary expressions of church structure and the subsequent practice of the pastoral offices.

Several distinct obstacles to unity and fulfillment of the Great Commission are before us as we move toward the conclusion of our earthly work:

- **Sectarianism.** The arrogance and partiality produced by excessive denominationalism, reinforced by entrenched dogmatism over non-essential beliefs and practices, presents the greatest obstacle to organic unity and completion of the primary task. Sectarianism has taught us to think and work independently while either aggressively attacking or simply ignoring significant segments of the church.
- **Modernism.**[15] After hundreds of years in which the church had pre-eminence in economic and social issues, education and the arts, modernism has effectively painted the church as intellectually deficient, culturally irrelevant and often the focus of ridicule and scorn, affecting even the theologians and clergy. Modernism has given rise to the secularization of once-Christian cultures and has promoted excessive individualism.
- **Anti-Semitism.** Rampant and often violent anti-Semitism has created profound resistance among the Jews and a

---

14. Excerpt from: Rex A. Koivisto, *One Lord, One Faith,* Victor Books/SP Publications, 1993, p. 137.
15. Modernism: the practice of subordinating traditional Christian teaching to contemporary thought (rationalism, higher criticism, philosophy and science) and especially diminishing its supernatural elements. Modernism, also referred to as neo-Protestantism, was popularized in the 1800s and has become the dominant approach to Christianity in higher education, business, government and the media. Modernism has given support to the increase of societal secularism and humanism.

wall of separation from our true spiritual roots as the heirs of promises made through Abraham, Isaac, Jacob, David and the prophets.

- **Racism.** In addition to the specific racism often expressed toward the Jews, the sin of racial prejudice of any category plagues our history and thwarts our progress. The American church is guilty of individual and institutional racism, especially against black Africans and their descendants. While it may be argued that the church is not directly involved in the ongoing support of racism, the black community could easily view the general lack of response to racial issues as a conspiracy of silence. From that viewpoint, direct or indirect racism presents little difference. This smoldering issue is one of the greatest barriers to the unified health of the church.

- **Universalism.**[16] This doctrine, which was officially repudiated long ago, is fast becoming the cultural religion of the day and is even re-emerging in the modern church, even among historically conservative evangelicals and Pentecostals. The lack of commonly recognized orthodoxy among all Christians, combined with an absence of modern authoritative apostolic church councils, undermines the potential for meaningful unity and cooperation.

God cannot be pleased with our current state with regard to these issues, since it is not consistent with His nature, promises, intent or ultimate purpose for His church. We cannot remain the way we are and accomplish His purposes, so

---

16. Universalist Unitarianism professes that there will be an "ultimate reconciliation" of all men to God at some future point, removing the need for people to be saved solely within this lifetime. There is a range of beliefs within this movement; some proclaim that even Satan ultimately will be reconciled to God. These teachings have a long history within the church, dating back as early as the writings of Origen. Both the Old and New Testaments teach eternal judgment for those outside of the covenants of God.

change must happen at every stratum of the church. Those entrusted with leadership on every level must point the way.

The restoration of a widely recognized apostolic office offers a very real opportunity for addressing some of these matters. True bishops should confront these issues individually and use their influence to sway others. The ability to call apostolic ecumenical councils that have broadly accepted authority is a primary key to fundamental change. Defining the role of bishops in the contemporary church is an important step in this process.

If we can have a better understanding of the pastoral offices and of how they relate to one another in a church of such diversity, then we may find new pathways to meaningful and lasting cooperation as we finish the task of taking the Gospel to "every creature."

Key Discussion Points:

1. The new reformation and its ramifications for unity and cooperation.
2. The restoration of the office of the apostle/bishop to the church at large.
3. The need for continuity with the ancient and universal church.
4. The establishment of broadly accepted standards of orthodoxy and ordination of the episcopate.

Questions:

1. Have you noticed in your church, denomination or movement a resurgence of interest in the roles of apostles and bishops?
2. Do you agree that there is a need for a system of accountability for bishops?
3. Can you name ways in which more accountability for Christian leaders would be beneficial?
4. Do you think that current accountability structures could be improved?

Chapter Eight

The Roles of Bishops in the Contemporary Church

The universal church, whether we are talking about a denomination, a local congregation of believers or a specialized parachurch ministry, must have recognized leadership. Whatever specific form or structure of leadership a group of Christians may adopt, it should be understood that the chosen leaders are, in fact, providing apostolic oversight as successors of the apostles. In other words, every biblically based system of oversight has roots in, and has been passed on to us through, the original apostles. Therefore, great care should be given to how leaders are chosen and how their leadership is exercised. Whether in historic apostolic succession or not, whether they are clergy or lay leaders, whether traditional or not, Christian leaders must recognize that they are acting as successors of the apostles of Christ.

A significant portion of the Protestant church does not recognize the validity of contemporary apostles. Like many of the early reformers,[1] they adamantly reject any continuing role of apostle, especially as characterized by the title or role of "bishop."

---

1. The leaders of the Protestant Reformation of the sixteenth century.

As discussed in the previous chapter, there is a worldwide resurgence of interest in the apostolic offices, but a lack of standards and systems for these emerging apostles. The potential positive effect upon the whole church as it recovers its apostolic roots and mission cannot be overstated. Since there is such a surge in discussion of the office of apostle, then we should examine biblical and historic examples of how it may be practiced effectively today and in the future. As pointed out earlier, the role of apostle was carried forth into the office of bishop while some of the original apostles were still alive. The transfer of the apostolic office from apostles to bishops was a bumpy process that occurred over the first century. The traditional office of bishop and its biblical forerunner, the office of apostle, provide insights for strengthening the role of modern-day apostles, and more important, a model for the apostolic call of every believer.

The traditional view among sacramental churches such as Roman Catholic or Anglican churches is that bishops in apostolic succession succeed *from* the apostles, but do not succeed *to* the office of an apostle. In other words, they would not expect modern-day bishops to actually be apostles in the biblical sense. This would explain why most bishops in churches that hold this view do not functionally minister in the biblical apostolic model, which emphasizes the extension of the church through evangelism, signs, wonders and apostolic teaching. They are more likely to act as pastoral guides and as organizational administrators to their jurisdictional clergy and churches.

Others, myself included, believe that the role of apostles is as important for the church today as it was in the New Testament. Since the office of bishop emerged from the New Testament period and has a two thousand year traceable history, it can serve as a model of understanding for the role of apostles in the modern church.

What, then, should be the role of bishops in the church today?

Four primary apostolic roles for bishops have been commonly acknowledged throughout the ages:

- "Guardians of Orthodoxy"
- "Administrators of the Sacraments"
- "Shepherds of the Flock"
- "Symbols of Unity"

While these are definitely needful roles for modern bishops as well, I would add a few others that are biblical roles the original apostles demonstrated. These additional roles include:

- "Advocates of the Great Commission"
- "Champions of Racial, Gender and Cultural Harmony"
- "Defenders of the Rights and Needs of the Poor"
- "Promoters of the Supernatural"
- "Agents of Societal Transformation"
- "Fathers of the Faith"

These vital roles that bishops fulfill are as needed today as at any point in history, whether practiced with the traditional symbolism that has long accompanied this office or not.

Before we continue, it must be stated again that the church of Jesus Christ is a community of faith, not a human corporation or government. The bishop is a fellow member and partaker of that community, not apart from it or above it. All believers are called into the continuing apostolic ministry of Christ on some level of support and participation. The role of bishops, like that of all clergy, leaders and members, is "from within" the community. Along with the episcopate, the bishop is to coach and teach from within the community of faith by example, so that the whole community may find its place of service and purpose.

As we consider these defined, specific roles of bishops, you may determine that these functions are the very same roles that *all* Christians should fulfill. In fact, every Christian *should* carry out these important functions to some degree. That is why it is essential for bishops, presbyters, deacons and all Christian leaders to comprehensively understand and convey to the contemporary church the apostolic ministry that has been biblically and historically understood and practiced. Bishops must take the lead and set an example and tone for others to follow, especially in working with pastors of local churches and leaders of Christian ministries.

Let us look further, then, at the required, traditional and biblical roles of bishops:

The Role of Bishops as Guardians of Orthodoxy

As a guardian of orthodoxy, a bishop is charged with maintaining continuity with historic Christian doctrine, especially as embodied in the teachings of the Old and New Testament and in the primary historical creeds. Therefore, a bishop must be well studied in Scripture, the creeds and church history. A bishop is an educator, so he must commit to a life of learning and teaching, especially to those in apostolic ministry. He is called to be one with the apostles in proclaiming and interpreting the Gospel of Christ and must pledge fidelity to the Holy Scriptures.

A bishop also must exemplify the virtue of study to all believers, especially to those in leadership. The apostle Paul's admonition to *"study to shew thyself approved unto God"*[2] is as needed today as it was when he challenged Timothy to a higher level of understanding.

The great author, pastor and teacher Dr. A.W. Tozer commented on the habit of study in his day among Christians in a series of articles in the *Alliance Weekly* on the subject "The Use and Abuse of Books." Dr. Tozer stated: "Why does today's Christian find the reading of great books always beyond him? Certainly intellectual powers do not wane from one generation to another. We are as smart as our fathers and any thought that they could entertain we can entertain if we are sufficiently interested to make the effort. The major cause of the decline in the quality of current Christian literature is not intellectual, but spiritual. To enjoy a great religious book requires a degree

---

2. 2 Timothy 2:15 (KJV).

of consecration to God and detachment from the world that few modern Christians have. The early Christian Fathers, the Mystics, the Puritans, are not hard to understand, but they inhabit the highlands where the air is crisp and rarefied, and none but the God-enamored can come."[3]

In his comments, Dr. Tozer connects true spirituality with the discipline of study. This is not the spiritless intellectualism that often plagues our higher thinking; rather, this is a hunger-driven yearning to comprehend deeper truths. Anyone who stands in the place of a teacher must have a deep commitment to study.

Dr. C. Peter Wagner is a qualified and highly regarded academic leader in the church. In an observation about the training model of what he refers to as the "New Apostolic Churches," he states: "Academic requirements for ordination, so long the staple in traditional churches, are being scrapped. New apostolic ordination is primarily rooted in personal relationships, which verify character, and in proven ministry skills."[4]

While I would be the first to agree that proven ministry anointing and personal relationships are indispensable and are far superior to educational degrees alone, there is still a fundamental need for scholarship among those who are to lead the flock of God. Can we afford to endure the years it will take for a pastor to explore every Bible truth and to develop a basic competency in his or her own understanding that might ultimately prove inadequate or even heretical? This question may sound absurd, since we generally expect these apostolic leaders to hold high standards of Bible proficiency. But we all have our stories. While the idea of less-formal, more-practical theological freshness portends many positives, the lack of formal training has already been proven to be problematic in several cases with which I have personal experience.

---

3. A.W. Tozer, "The Use and Abuse of Books" article written for *Alliance Weekly,* February 22, 1956, p. 2.
4. C. Peter Wagner, *The New Apostolic Churches,* Regal Books, Ventura, California, 1998, p. 21.

Consider how God combined the anointing of the apostle Paul with the extensive educational background he possessed. Though he was taught by *"revelation,"*[5] God used Paul's theological training to give to his writings, above all of the other New Testament writers, the greatest texture and understanding of the Gospel in the context of the historical covenants, God's eternal plan and the promises to the patriarchs. We cannot imagine the New Testament without the Spirit-inspired insights of this great theologian.

There simply must be a higher educational standard for those in the pastoral offices, for they are the primary teachers. Though formal degrees are not an absolute necessity, higher study is not optional.

A bishop must hold the study and orthodoxy standards high for all.

The Role of Bishops as Administrators of the Sacraments

As the administrator of the sacraments, a bishop is to provide for the proper use of the sacraments as characterized in Scripture. In this role the bishop is called to superintend the shared administration of the sacraments with other ministers. This role also brings to the forefront the role of bishops in the appointment and training of leaders into the apostolic ministry of Christ.

In Exodus, we see an example of how even the most common elements can be made holy. *"'Do not come any closer,' God said. 'Take off your sandals, for the place where you are standing is holy ground.'"*[6] Simply stated, God's presence makes the material holy. Thus, we have a basis for understanding the sacraments. Not only is God holy, He makes the material holy. He, in fact, gives us certain places, days, observances and symbols that are to be *"holy to the LORD."*[7]

---

5. Ephesians 3:3.
6. Exodus 3:5.
7. Exodus 30:10.

Christian worship contains biblically based rites in which God is uniquely active. Historically, these rites have been called "sacraments." Though the number of officially sanctioned sacraments has varied depending on the branch of the church, the existence of sacraments has been almost universally recognized. The word *sacrament* comes from the combination of two latin words: *sacra*, which means "holy" and *mentum*, which means "to make." Thus, the word *sacrament* literally means "to make holy." In the *Concise Dictionary of Religion* from InterVarsity Press, a sacrament is defined as "a rite in which God is uniquely active." Most of the church throughout history has held that there are certain rites and signs that are singularly given by God to the church. And when these rites are practiced, a grace and holy presence of God is manifest within them that may be experienced only through these sacramental acts.

The least ritualistic practice of the sacraments is generally found among evangelicals, who primarily view them as "ordinances." In this way of thinking, ordinances are intended to be practiced as dutiful obedience to a biblical directive rather than as moments in which God is uniquely active. There is a broad view concerning ordinances among different segments of Protestantism. Generally speaking, the evangelical view is that a participant in an ordinance should not expect any "mystical presence" such as a special grace of God imparted as the ordinance is practiced. While sacramentalists consider ordinances and sacraments as *means* of grace, evangelicals consider them *signs* of grace. Yet even for the most ardent evangelical, there is more to these acts than mere symbolism. Many will readily admit that something more occurs during the performance of ordinances, though they are usually hard-pressed to explain how it may be so or just what it is.

Take baptism, for example. Is there only an outward symbolism occurring during a baptism, or is there an impartation of some inward spiritual blessing? Is there a measure of God's presence or a unique grace attached to that moment? Most would agree that something more lasting than mere symbolic obedience transpires. This "something more" is what sacramentalism is all about. It is a belief that there is an inward spiritual grace experienced during an outward symbolic act that is sanctioned by Scripture. From a sacramentalist point of view, a sacrament is not mere symbolism, but a sign of God's imparted grace. Plainly stated, the sacraments of baptism or Communion are not simply symbols or ordinances of obedience when done in true faith, but rites and signs through which we receive an inward grace from God that is unique to that act.

I once was in a Baptist church where our youth group was to put on a performance for the entire congregation. We busily began preparing the stage by removing plants, chairs and other items. When we were poised to move the pulpit, the pastor adamantly explained that this would not be permitted because "the pulpit is where the Word of God is preached, therefore it is holy." Though hardly sacramental from a liturgical perspective, this evangelical pastor revealed the conflict felt by many in this branch of the church. He was unknowingly acting sacramentally. He was admitting to a special presence of God upon an instrument of preaching. Years later, preaching in a Pentecostal church, I turned my back to the pulpit while making an illustration. In doing so, I unknowingly offended the pastor, who later explained that I "should not turn my backside to a holy thing." He would probably be shocked, and perhaps even further insulted, if he were to be told that he, too, was acting sacramentally. He professed by his actions a belief that God can make a material thing holy when it is set apart for His purposes. Both of these examples demonstrate that even the most strident anti-symbolism and anti-sacramentalistic Christians can be quite symbolic and sacramental.

If you consider yourself an enlightened charismatic, you might say upon hearing these two stories, "Well, contemporary, biblically sound charismatics and Pentecostals wouldn't be so errant." Perhaps, but let me put it this way—who else but a self-described *non-sacramental* charismatic or Pentecostal would lay hands on an unoccupied chair and believe for a touch of God for the next person who sits in it? Non-sacramental? Hardly. Let me offer another example. Most Pentecostals would readily support praying over pieces of cloth to be given to others for the purpose of healing or blessing. The evangelical or even the sacramentalist may balk at this practice, but isn't a similar practice found in the New Testament? *"God did extraordinary miracles through Paul. Handkerchiefs and aprons that had touched him were taken to the sick, and their illnesses were cured and the evil spirits left them."*[8] Though evangelicals, Pentecostals and charismatics generally view the historical sacraments non-sacramentally, they *act* sacramentally in many of their church practices.

Perhaps the problem is more a lack of understanding of true sacramentalism than actual disbelief in it. There are legitimate concerns that practicing sacramentalism may draw our attention to symbolism and rituals instead of to God Himself. But singing, giving, hearing sermons and personal prayer are other practices that have the potential to become mere rituals. Any biblical act of worship may develop into meaningless ritual if one has a nonchalant attitude or separates worship practices from a personal commitment to Christ and a daily yielding to the Person and work of the Holy Spirit. We must practice the things we do in worship in faith toward God and expectation of His powerful presence lest they become nothing more than lifeless routine.

Let us again refer to the simple yet profound definition of a sacrament provided by St. Augustine: a sacrament is "an outward and visible sign of an inward and invisible grace." The idea behind the recognition of specific sacraments is that God works through perceptible and visible signs. These signs are tangible meeting points between God and man. Common examples of this kind of "meeting point" are Communion, baptism, marriage, laying on of hands, anointing with oil, preaching, teaching or publicly reading the Word of God.

---

8. Acts 19:11-12.

These are all points of intersection between the action of God and the faith of man. So, Communion, as an example, is not simply a symbolic ritual, but a divine moment of God being invisibly present in visible, tangible, biblical worship. Therefore, in sacramental worship, one can expect an inward work of grace unique to that rite—a true presence of Christ that can be experienced by no other means. The very act of gathering together as the people of God in the name of Jesus is a sacramental experience unduplicated in even the most devout private, personal devotion. In Matthew 18:20 we read, *"'For where two or three come together in my name, there am I with them.'"* This presence of Christ promised to those who gather in His name is precisely the kind of grace experienced in performing a sacramental act.

By going beyond the generally recognized short list of baptism and Communion, I am revealing my own viewpoint— that there is a true presence of Christ and a unique impartation of grace that accompanies all of these observances. If I were to number the sacraments, I would extend them to include all of the biblical rites given uniquely to the church. But for common practice of the whole church, the traditionally recognized sacraments of baptism and the Holy Eucharist suffice.

As we celebrate Communion as a sacrament, we can expect a true presence of Christ that is unique to this rite. It is not merely symbolic. It is not just an act of obedience as an ordinance. It is a time of impartation of God's grace. The same is true for baptism. He is present in these sacraments, and we will be changed by observing them. His presence always makes a difference.

So, if a rite or sign can be holy, can a person, place or thing be holy? The historically sacramental churches would answer with a resounding "yes." Evangelicals, however, would typically resist this idea, properly citing the need for biblical evidence, preferably from the New Testament. Let's look at several New Testament examples of people, places and things being made holy:

- 1 Corinthians 6:19 states: *"Do you not know that your body is a temple of the Holy Spirit, who is in you, whom you have received from God? You are not your own."* Here is a case of a human body being made sacred. We are not only inwardly holy, but the physical bodies of believers are declared to be temples, and therefore they are holy unto the Lord.

- In Ephesians 3:5, the apostle Paul affirms that there is a sacredness in the positions of prophet and apostle as he speaks of the mystery of Christ that the spirit has revealed *"to God's holy apostles and prophets."* In fact, it can be argued that anytime God declares a person "holy" and therefore "sets him apart" for a unique work, there is a special grace and anointing from God that is distinct from the holiness we each possess as Christians.

- Luke 10:5-6 declares: *"'And into whatsoever house ye enter, first say, Peace be to this house. And if the son of peace be there, your peace shall rest upon it: if not, it shall turn to you again'"* (KJV). It is clear that a tangible presence of God is being given or withdrawn in this passage. It is not speaking simply of the peace of God that is brought to a home as long as a Christian resides there. Jesus speaks of an imparted peace that we ourselves have the authority to speak over a place. If the "son of peace" is present, our spoken peace will remain. If not, it will be returned to us. From this passage we can infer that we have authority from God to bless a material place in His name.

- In Revelation 21:10 we read, *"And he carried me away in the Spirit to a mountain great and high, and showed me the Holy City, Jerusalem, coming down out of heaven from God."* Heaven is an entirely sacred place. All that is present there and all that emanates from it is holy unto the Lord. We, too, are now seated in heavenly places in Christ Jesus. Our lives, our labors and all that we possess are to be holy unto God.

In each of these passages we see people, places and things declared as sacred or changed by God's presence. Other examples of holy things in the New Testament are *"Holy Scriptures"* in Romans 1:2 and 2 Timothy 3:15, *"holy hands"* in 1 Timothy 2:8, *"the sacred mountain"* (mountain of transfiguration) in 2 Peter 1:18, and even a *"holy kiss"* in 1 Thessalonians 5:26. God's presence is not limited to a single form of manifestation, but is manifest in many unique ways. These New Testament examples are in addition to the multitude of Old Testament examples of God declaring many things, such as days, people, places, objects and acts of worship, as holy.

It is a self-evident truth that as people diminish the value of the sacred, they lose some of their spiritual discipline. Yet when people honor that which God has made holy, their faith and actions are invigorated, and discipline and godliness follow. For instance, in 1 Corinthians 6:19-20 we read: *"Do you not know that your body is a temple of the Holy Spirit, who is in you, whom you have received from God? You are not your own; you were bought at a price. Therefore honor God with your body."* In this passage, the apostle Paul connects recognition of a holy thing, one's body in this case, to the motivation to behave righteously. A Christian culture that has little appreciation for holy things, places or moments breeds a lack of spiritual discipline. To the extent a casual attitude toward holy things prevails, a casual attitude toward personal holiness often manifests itself as well. Strangely, overfamiliarity is an uninvited companion that often accompanies the liberty and intimacy with God often experienced in true worship. We presume more than we should.

God's presence is intimate, special and welcoming. He greets us with open arms and grants us acceptance on the basis of that which Christ has done for us. As He receives us into His presence, we must be careful to maintain a sense of awe and respect for His greatness and majesty, never taking for granted this opportunity to *"enter his gates."*[9] It is only by grace that we enter.

---

9. Psalm 100:4.

It is only by His conscious decision to turn His wrath away from our sin and disobedience by placing it on our Savior that we may stand in His presence. A nonchalant, overfamiliar casualness should never characterize our approach to God. He is holy.

The practice of the sacraments historically has been given the same consideration as the preaching and teaching ministry or the spiritual leadership of the church. While some contend that all believers have an equal right to the oversight and management of all of these things, most branches of the church have held that the practice of the sacraments, along with the oversight of the teaching ministry and the spiritual leadership, should be done by those who have been recognized, trained and ordained to do so. At the very least, biblical formats and words must be adhered to and those entrusted with these rights held accountable.

If, then, God considers people, places, rites and things holy and His Word declares people, places, rites and things holy, we also should treat the gathering of God's church and the sacramental things we do in obedience to Him as holy. Perhaps in doing so, we can restore a sense of reverence and honor for God into our lives and worship that is so often lacking in the church today.

As administrator of the sacraments, a bishop must help maintain an understanding of the sacraments and provide for their regular administration.

The Role of Bishops as Shepherds of the Flock

The bishop is to provide a good example of faithfulness and purity to God's holy flock. He must obey Jesus' command to "*feed my sheep*"[10] and the apostle Paul's admonition to "*Guard yourselves and all the flock of which the Holy Spirit has made you overseers. Be shepherds of the church of God, which he bought with his own blood.*"[11] All Christians who

---

10. John 21:15-18.
11. Acts 20:28.

care for the flock of God in any capacity are cooperating assistant shepherds working in partnership with and as an extension of the Chief Shepherd, our Lord Jesus Christ. To keep from becoming too controlling of God's flock, we must maintain a right perspective. It is God's flock, not our own.

The starting point for those who desire to fulfill the command to be shepherds of others is for they themselves to *"have returned to the Shepherd and Overseer of [their] souls."*[12] Though we may be shepherds indeed, we also are sheep. Part of our responsibility is to help the flock of God discover that they, too, are potential shepherds.

The care of God's flock is shared by all believers. But while every Christian can and should care for one another, bishops, along with all Christian leaders, are directly and forcefully commanded to carry forth the ministry of shepherding God's flock after the example of Christ, the Chief Shepherd. Therefore bishops must *"be shepherds of God's flock that is under your care, serving as overseers—not because you must, but because you are willing, as God wants you to be; not greedy for money, but eager to serve; not lording it over those entrusted to you, but being examples to the flock. And when the Chief Shepherd appears, you will receive the crown of glory that will never fade away."*[13]

The tendency for bishops to become primarily administrators instead of pastors has led to many of the problems we have seen both historically and currently. The office of bishop, as practiced in the primitive church, was directly tied to local and translocal ministry, in the tradition of the early apostles. A bishop who loses connection with the role of shepherd of the flock of God has departed from legitimate fulfillment of this vital office.

The people of God have less need for an administrator than for a true leader who will pastorally and prophetically act

---

12. 1 Peter 2:25.
13. 1 Peter 5:2-4.

on their behalf. It requires less of a personal commitment to holiness and genuine spirituality to be an administrative leader than to be a spiritual example and shepherd of the flock. For this reason, many in apostolic ministry prefer to lean more in the direction of an organizational leader than a shepherd.

A shepherd is not a *ruler*, but a *servant* of the flock. The biblical pattern of leadership is clear: *"Jesus called them together and said, 'You know that the rulers of the Gentiles lord it over them, and their high officials exercise authority over them. Not so with you. Instead, whoever wants to become great among you must be your servant, and whoever wants to be first must be your slave—just as the Son of Man did not come to be served, but to serve, and to give his life as a ransom for many.'"*[14] Bishops, along with all who represent the apostolic ministry on any level, should be shepherds of the flock above all other leadership roles. The need and deepest desire in the heart of God's sheep toward their leaders is reflected in this biblical prayer: *"'May the LORD, the God of the spirits of all mankind, appoint a man over this community to go out and come in before them, one who will lead them out and bring them in, so the LORD's people will not be like sheep without a shepherd.'"*[15]

A bishop must provide an example of a true shepherd to the episcopate and to all of the people of God.

The Role of Bishops as Symbols of Unity

The unity of the church is absolutely dependent upon the person and work of the Holy Spirit. However, we also have a significant part in this work. For this reason, the apostle Paul encouraged us to *"make every effort to keep the unity of the Spirit through the bond of peace."*[16]

Our efforts are eased by the apostolic office of bishop. The original apostles and later the bishops provided a "sign" or "symbol" of unity for the church at large. The Rev. Canon

---

14. Matthew 20:25-28.
15. Numbers 27:15-17.
16. Ephesians 4:3.

Professor Richard A. Norris Jr. notes, "In being a 'sign of unity,' then, the bishop, as teacher, pastor, and liturgical president, is a servant of the original 'apostolic faith.'"[17]

As a symbol of unity, the bishop must have a catholic (universal) view of the church and actively promote fellowship and strategic cooperation among all Christians. He must have a love and embrace of the church of history, the church of today and the church of eternity. He must be willing to take counsel together with fellow bishops and share with companion presbyters in the governance and oversight of the whole church. "In Cyprian (St. Cyprian, bishop of Carthage, 200-258 A.D.) as well as the North African church of at least a generation before his day, we find an emphasis on the need for bishops to meet together and reach a 'common mind' under the Spirit's guidance."[18]

With such divisions as we see in the church today, we need symbols of unity now more than ever. The Great Commission is our "purpose" unifier, but by what means shall we tangibly work together? Modern conferences and gatherings have provided some relief of our divisions, and many meaningful alliances and cooperative efforts have resulted from them. But where do we go from here? Historically, God has used councils of bishops to forge unity and to protect the church from heresy. While many successful efforts have been made to reinstate some form of church councils, the modern evangelical and Pentecostal/charismatic branches of the church catholic generally have been bypassed in this process, mostly by their own choice and design.

This is a new day in which we live. Our problems and situations are new, but many of the solutions are as old as history itself. The contemporary unfolding of the office of bishop

---

17. Richard A. Norris, Jr., from a paper on *"Bishops, Succession, and the Apostolicity of the Church,"* published as a chapter in *On Being a Bishop,* The Church Hymnal Corporation, New York, 1993, p. 53.

18. J. Robert Wright, *The Ministry of Bishops: A Study Document Authorized by the House of Bishops of the Episcopal Church,* published by Trinity Institute, Trinity Parish, New York, 1991.

beyond the nature of its practice since the Reformation is one key among several that will unlock visible unity in the church of Jesus Christ.

The bishop must be a symbol and active champion of unity.

The Role of Bishops as
Advocates of the Great Commission

To fulfill the role of advocate of the Great Commission, a bishop must have an apostolic viewpoint and commitment to finish the task of world evangelization. The apostolic vision of the church begins with Jesus' declaration that *"'this gospel of the kingdom will be preached in the whole world as a testimony to all nations, and then the end will come.'"*[19] The authentic bishop's intent is to stand in heaven, having been a full participant in helping to make happen what is now beheld: *"After this I looked and there before me was a great multitude that no one could count, from every nation, tribe, people and language, standing before the throne and in front of the Lamb. They were wearing white robes and were holding palm branches in their hands. And they cried out in a loud voice: 'Salvation belongs to our God, who sits on the throne, and to the Lamb.' All the angels were standing around the throne and around the elders and the four living creatures. They fell down on their faces before the throne and worshiped God, saying: 'Amen! Praise and glory and wisdom and thanks and honor and power and strength be to our God for ever and ever. Amen!'"*[20]

The role of advocate of the primary task of the church on the earth may be the most important for a bishop. Traditionally, it is often only the missionary force and its relatively few supporters who continually wave the banner for the Great Commission. Why should the apostolicity of the church be advocated only by a few who are directly engaged in it? If the role of bishop is in any sense the ongoing role of apostle

---

19. Matthew 24:14.
20. Revelation 7:9-12.

within the church, then it should be the bishops above all who promote the clarion call to finish the task. Local churches, along with their leaders and members, often struggle along without clear purpose or direction. A local church, or for that matter an individual Christian, will languish listlessly and not enjoy the delightful experience of purpose and destiny while disconnected from the Great Commission. But authentic shepherds will not permit the people of God over which God has made them overseers to be ignorant of the centrality of the Great Commission or severed from a vital connection to it.

A true bishop is dedicated to the salvation and discipling of all nations through active, universal fulfillment of the Great Commission.

The Role of Bishops as Champions of Racial, Gender and Cultural Harmony

Christ Himself gave us an example of overcoming racial, gender and cultural prejudice in His ministry to the woman at the well.[21] The very words of the woman, along with the commentary of the apostle John, demonstrate how Jesus defied prejudices: *"The Samaritan woman said to him, 'You are a Jew and I am a Samaritan woman. How can you ask me for a drink?' (For Jews do not associate with Samaritans.)"*[22] Men customarily did not talk to married women in public. Jesus' disciples were amazed at this seeming lack of discretion: *"Just then his disciples returned and were surprised to find him talking with a woman. But no one asked, 'What do you want?' or 'Why are you talking with her?'"*[23] Even more surprising than the gender issue was the fact that Jesus was talking to a *Samaritan* woman. The Jews despised Samaritans and avoided them. But there was no love lost on either side of this conflict. In fact, when the Samaritans in one village heard that Jesus was

---

21. John 4:7-27.
22. John 4:9.
23. John 4:27.

on his way to Jerusalem, the city of the Jews, they wanted nothing to do with Him.[24] The disciples wanted to call down fire from heaven to punish them. This would seem like an overreaction if the long-standing ire between Jews and Samaritans were not taken into account. When the Pharisees wanted to demean Jesus in the eyes of the Jewish people, they accused Him of being "demon-possessed" and, even worse, "a Samaritan."[25] Jesus attacked these prejudices on several occasions by ministering openly to Samaritans[26] and by using a Samaritan as the hero of one of His most famous parables.[27] Jesus made it a regular part of His ministry to confront hypocrisy and prejudices.

The first step toward Christ that would eventually lead him into his apostolic call required that Nathanael confront his *regional* prejudice. *"Philip found Nathanael and told him, 'We have found the one Moses wrote about in the Law, and about whom the prophets also wrote—Jesus of Nazareth, the son of Joseph.' 'Nazareth! Can anything good come from there?' Nathanael asked. 'Come and see,' said Philip."*[28] Nathanael himself was from Galilee, another region that often experienced prejudicial contempt, yet he now asked *"'Can anything good come from [Nazareth]?'"*

Was this insecurity or arrogance? Our prejudices have many roots. In his classic book *The Training of the Twelve*, Dr. A.B. Bruce gives insight into this story: "While Nathanael was not free from prejudices, he showed guilelessness in being willing to have them removed. He came and saw. This openness to conviction is the mark of moral integrity. The guileless man dogmatizes not, but investigates, and therefore always comes right in the end. The man of bad, dishonest heart, on the contrary, does not come and see. Deeming it in his interest to remain in his

---

24. Luke 9:51-56.
25. John 8:48.
26. Luke 17:11-19.
27. Luke 10:25-37.
28. John1:45-46.

present mind, he studiously avoids looking at aught which does not tend to confirm his foregone conclusions."[29]

The apostle Peter was forced to confront his own bigotry in his vision on the rooftop and his subsequent ministry to the Gentile Cornelius.[30] The Jews considered Gentiles to be *"unclean"* in their practices[31] and objects of *"reproach."*[32] That God would pour out His Spirit upon Gentile converts was astounding to the early Jewish believers; indeed, this truth practically had to be forced upon them. Peter's comments are very revealing: *"I now realize how true it is that God does not show favoritism but accepts men from every nation who fear him and do what is right."*[33] Until that moment of realization, Peter had been as prejudiced against all Gentiles as any Jew of his day. It was only through revelation provoked by a vision that he began to see clearly in this matter.

His first order of business, after his own epiphany, was to enlighten the other apostles and believers, since they were still steeped in their prejudices. Consider their words as they reveal their attitude toward Gentiles: *"The apostles and the brothers throughout Judea heard that the Gentiles also had received the word of God. So when Peter went up to Jerusalem, the circumcised believers criticized him and said, 'You went into the house of uncircumcised men and ate with them.'"*[34] Only after hearing a full description of the events did they change their attitude. *"When they heard this, they had no further objections and praised God, saying, 'So then, God has granted even the Gentiles repentance unto life.'"*[35] This whole incident is an excellent example of God using apostolic influence to impact general prejudices in God's people.

---

29. A.B. Bruce, *The Training of the Twelve*, Kregel Publications, Grand Rapids, Michigan 1971, p. 7.
30. Acts 10:1-48.
31. Ezra 6:21.
32. Nehemiah 5:9.
33. Acts 10:34.
34. Acts 11:1-3.
35. Acts 11:18.

The apostle Paul, in his apostolic teaching and leadership role, declared: *"There is neither Jew nor Greek, slave nor free, male nor female, for you are all one in Christ Jesus,"*[36] and again, *"Here there is no Greek or Jew, circumcised or uncircumcised, barbarian, Scythian, slave or free, but Christ is all, and is in all."*[37] His ensuing cross-cultural call from God and ministry to the Gentiles[38] demonstrate that the apostolic example must be one of confronting and overcoming racism or intolerance and modeling Christian conciliation through the Gospel.

While the Holy Scriptures certainly confront specific human behaviors that are to be condemned, and Christians in their role as *"light"* in the world also must confront these behaviors, we must never allow our condemnation of sin to become a hatred for sinners. Jesus cannot be legitimately accused of toleration of sin, yet He consistently stood against cultural or religious exclusion of those who were sinners or of those who were objects of racial, ethnic or other types of prejudice.

Christ and His apostles point the way for bishops to demonstrate the proper role of the whole church in matters of prejudice.

The Role of Bishops as Defenders of the Rights and Needs of the Poor, the Broken and the Imprisoned

When Paul and Barnabas went before James, Peter and John for confirmation of their apostolic ministry to the Gentiles, they received only one direct counsel: *"that we should continue to remember the poor, the very thing I was eager to do."*[39] The "pillars" of the church had this value, Paul was "eager" to remember the poor, and James wrote about this vital ministry in his letter.[40] Jesus declared ministry to the poor to

---

36. Galatians 3:28.
37. Colossians 3:11.
38. Acts 13:47.
39. Galatians 2:10.
40. James 2:2-6.

be one of the hallmarks of His ministry when He said, *"'The Spirit of the* LORD *is on me, because he has anointed me to preach good news to the poor. He has sent me to proclaim freedom for the prisoners and recovery of sight for the blind, to release the oppressed, to proclaim the year of the* LORD*'s favor.'"*[41] The feeding of the five thousand[42] and the four thousand[43] demonstrated Jesus' personal compassion for the hungry and showed that He wanted to teach the disciples to follow His example. The role of Christians is not only to preach the Gospel, but to minister to broken humanity's physical and emotional needs. The story of Jesus forgiving the prostitute[44] shows that He was compassionate to and forgave the most broken of transgressors, all the while being criticized for being a *"'friend of the tax collectors and sinners.'"*[45]

The apostle Paul used his apostolic influence to seek benevolence from all the churches where he had sway to meet the physical needs of those in Jerusalem who were experiencing famine. His comments in 2 Corinthians 8:11-15 demonstrate his belief that we have a universal responsibility to give to those in need, while not unduly burdening anyone: *"Now finish the work, so that your eager willingness to do it may be matched by your completion of it, according to your means. For if the willingness is there, the gift is acceptable according to what one has, not according to what he does not have. Our desire is not that others might be relieved while you are hard pressed, but that there might be equality. At the present time your plenty will supply what they need, so that in turn their plenty will supply what you need. Then there will be equality, as it is written: 'He that gathered much did not have too much, and he that gathered little did not have too little.'"* This same value was expressed by Paul's disciple, Titus: *"I thank God,*

---

41. Luke 4:19.
42. Matthew 14:14-21.
43. Matthew 15:32-38.
44. Luke 7:37-50.
45. Luke 7:34.

who put into the heart of Titus the same concern I have for you. For Titus not only welcomed our appeal, but he is coming to you with much enthusiasm and on his own initiative."[46] Paul, Titus and the other brothers involved in this collection also were engaged in the distribution of the funds.[47] This "hands-on" involvement is another demonstration of the importance to the apostle Paul of setting an example for the believers in Corinth with regard to benevolence.

The apostle James, with his typical flair for clarity, defines the true meaning of religious behavior practiced with biblical purity when he states, *"Religion that God our Father accepts as pure and faultless is this: to look after orphans and widows in their distress and to keep oneself from being polluted by the world."*[48]

Therefore, the bishop in the apostolic tradition must defend the rights and needs of those who are least able to defend themselves. The apostolic call is to lead by example and assure that everyone has the opportunity to hear and enjoy the full benefits of the Gospel, and to encourage all Christians to engage in this important witness for Christ.

The Role of Bishops as Promoters of the Supernatural

Jesus used miracles in His ministry to the masses, but He also specifically established an example of miracles among His disciples. The apostle John revealed, *"Jesus did many other miraculous signs in the presence of his disciples, which are not recorded in this book."*[49] The disciples paid close attention to the model that Jesus gave them, and they themselves were empowered by God to perform extraordinary signs and wonders during their ministry with Jesus on the earth and after His Ascension. Miracles were so identified with apostolic ministry that they became one of the signs of a true apostle. As the apostle Paul

---

46. 2 Corinthians 8:16-17.
47. 2 Corinthians 8:18-21.
48. James 1:27.
49. John 20:30.

asserts, *"The things that mark an apostle—signs, wonders and miracles—were done among you with great perserverance."*[50]

Churches should be places where the miraculous is commonplace. But not only should the *gathering of the believers* manifest the signs and wonders of God, these signs should follow the individual believers into their daily lives: *"'And these signs will accompany those who believe: In my name they will drive out demons; they will speak in new tongues; they will pick up snakes with their hands; and when they drink deadly poison, it will not hurt them at all; they will place their hands on sick people, and they will get well.'"*[51] The apostle Paul did not try to limit the use of signs and wonders among the churches; quite the opposite, he encouraged their orderly use, especially those supernatural gifts that built up the church or witnessed the power of the Gospel to the lost.

Since the church is *"built on the foundation of the apostles and prophets, with Christ Jesus himself as the chief cornerstone,"*[52] bishops must assure a proper foundation by allowing for and encouraging the supernatural, prophetic voice of God to come forth in all of its biblical methods. While it should be expected that the bishop, as with all Christian leaders who are in the teaching ministry, be prophetic, he also should encourage the biblical gift and office of prophetic utterance.

The Old Testament role of the prophet is not a complete model for the church today because there were no apostles in the Old Testament who, in God's system of order, could oversee the work of the prophet as in the New Testament: *"And in the church God has appointed first of all apostles, second prophets, third teachers, then workers of miracles, also those having gifts of healing, those able to help others, those with gifts of administration, and those speaking in different kinds of tongues."*[53] However, to better understand the functions of a

---

50. 2 Corinthians 12:12.
51. Mark 16:17-28.
52. Ephesians 2:20.
53. 1 Corinthians 12:28.

prophet, we should look to the Old Testament for guidance. H.I. Hester writes: "There are three Hebrew words translated 'prophet.' The first two of these are from the verb *Ro'eh*, used eleven times, and *Chozeh*, used twenty-two times. These words mean 'to see' and convey the idea of a man of vision. Thus the prophet is called a 'seer.' This implies that he is able to obtain a knowledge of spiritual realities not available to others. The third word *Nabhi*, used some three-hundred times, meaning to 'announce' or perhaps to 'bubble up,' represents the prophet as a 'speaker.'"[54] While the prophetic voice of God may indeed come forth in various manners in the church today, there is clearly a biblical mandate for both the gift and office of the prophet. Although we are still learning how these gifts and offices work together as we move forward toward our end-time role as the church, this important ministry of the prophetic must be promoted by those in apostolic office.

The volume of usage in the Old Testament of the word *nabhi*, which primarily has been associated with preaching, has led many scholars and theologians, especially in the more evangelical branches of the church, to determine that *preaching* is a sufficient provision of the prophetic voice of God for the church today, and therefore, there is no continuing role for prophets. For the most part, the same evangelicals are of the opinion that there is no role for bishops in the reformational church and no place for regular manifestation of the supernatural. Intellectualism and tradition without the balance of the supernatural, just like any other over-dependence of the flesh, can lead us down a path about which the apostle Paul warned us: *"having a form of godliness but denying its power."*[55]

Of course, the exercise of supernatural gifts can easily degrade into prideful showmanship, judgmental arrogance or disorderly conduct in those who practice them. The first letter to the Corinthian church provides us with a great example of

---

54. H. I. Hester, *The Heart of Hebrew History*, Broadman Press, Nashville, Tennessee, 1949, p. 273.
55. 2 Timothy 3:5.

an apostle bringing correction to the use of charismatic enablements without attempting to diminish the practice of the supernatural. Paul's counsel was that the Corinthians needed a comprehensive view of how the gifts were being practiced and how they impacted both believers and non-believers. Rather than counseling them to avoid the difficulties that the balanced use of the supernatural can present to leaders in the church, he simply reminded them that *"everything should be done in a fitting and orderly way."*[56]

Therefore, those called as bishops, who carry forth apostolic ministry to this generation and beyond should promote by example the ministry of the supernatural in all of its biblical forms and assure the orderly use of these supernatural enablements.

The Role of Bishops as Agents of Societal Transformation

A role that bishops in particular and Christian leaders in general have long fulfilled in society is that of agents of transformation. The very nature and message of the Gospel challenges, provokes and modifies secular society. Moral values, ethics, institutional sins, even cultural direction are issues that authentic Christianity confronts.

Throughout history, beginning with the Old Testament prophets and leaders, godly men and women, be they bishops, pastors or laypeople, have held positions of influence in society. Paul used his influence as an apostle of Christ, *plus* his background as a Pharisee,[57] as a Jew from a prominent Roman city[58] and as a Roman citizen,[59] and his superb theological training under a highly respected teacher of the law[60] to persuade others for Christ. In addition, many of the early martyrs

---

56. 1 Corinthians 14:40.
57. Philippians 3:5.
58. Acts 21:39.
59. Acts 22:25-28.
60. Acts 5:34; Acts 22:3.

were bishops. They were willing to stand up to the secular and religious structures of their day.

Why should the modern church abdicate its unique moral role in the human community? To some extent, especially in the more conservative, evangelical branches of the church, we have become so "eternity minded" that we have permitted those of immoral ilk to seize the social, political, educational and cultural high ground while we complain about the lack of Christian principles within these important influences. Instead of getting actively involved, we have become satisfied to float along like flotsam and jetsam on a cultural sea of outrageous behavior.

The cultures in which Christians live around the world are desperate for spiritual, moral leadership. Local, national and international crises or tragedies regularly reveal both the need and desire for spiritual input and pastoral care. The church must be "present and counted" in those moments of unique opportunity rather than "cloistered away" waiting for this present world to elapse. All too often, we show up to minister only to turn away again when it comes to the daily grind of responding to the human needs around us. The world notices.

The role of the church in demonstrating the Incarnation is as needed as ever. Bishops must be willing to take the lead, use available influence and urge all Christians to continually transform the culture and society around us by our active involvement and demonstration of divine love.

The Role of Bishops as Fathers of the Faith

There is a common tendency in the church to depend more upon a structural, governmental organization than a relational organization. To counter this, bishops must provide a model to the church of "fatherhood" rather than governmental or organizational executive leadership.

The best model for the church is a family. While healthy families have both governmental and organizational structure, the organic nature of a family causes the governmental and organizational elements to function differently than in other human institutions. At the head of this institution is the "father."

God reveals Himself to mankind in many ways. He is described as our "head,"[61] as the "Ruler, the King of kings and Lord of lords,"[62] and as our "Father."[63] The latter title puts God's governmental role as Ruler, King and Lord in an entirely different light. No longer can we relate to Him only from an organizational point of view; we must acknowledge the superiority of our organic, family connection to Him. While the apostle Paul was apt to point out his spiritual authority as an apostle, he characterized his role as that of a "father" to those over whom he exercised pastoral care. He said: "*I am not writing this to shame you, but to warn you, as my dear children. Even though you have ten thousand guardians in Christ, you do not have many fathers, for in Christ Jesus I became your father through the gospel. Therefore I urge you to imitate me.*"[64] Rather than imposing organizationally instituted obedience to a "guardian," he appealed to them to "imitate" him just as children would imitate their father.

Many of the initial bishops of the church are now considered to be "church fathers." Likewise, Abraham is often mentioned as a "father"[65] in his role to Israel and the church.

Perhaps now as never before, there is a cry for true spiritual "fathers" throughout the church worldwide. Our current organizational church and ministry structures cannot provide the needed connection, encouragement and accountability that organic, family-like relationships offer.

Bishops must provide an example and thereby assist all Christian leaders to emphasize the superiority of our organic connection with one another to our organizational connection. Since organizational unity is not likely to completely appear in the church prior to the second advent of Christ, our only hope of achieving true unity as we work toward the final harvest is an increased awareness of our familial connection to one another.

---

61. Colossians 2:10.
62. 1 Timothy 6:15.
63. 1 John 3:1.
64. 1 Corinthians 4:14-16.
65. Genesis 17:5; Romans 4:16.

Function Over Form

We have considered many of the important roles for bishops in the church today. As we deliberate the contemporary role of bishops, we remain challenged by the confusing and often discouraging two-thousand-year history of bishops and clergy, which includes everything from biblically modeled, legitimately practiced apostolic ministry to the most outrageous and scandalous examples of apostasy. By whatever means we address these issues we will face many difficulties.

The key to overcoming the negative models we have all seen and the doctrinal or historical confusion with which we still grapple is to return to the biblical *purpose* of those who shepherd the flock of God. Their appropriate *function* as shepherds is far superior to their *form* of selection or rank of ministry.

With regard to the importance of bishops and the clergy they ordain being in historic apostolic succession, it is my personal conviction that apostolic tradition (that is, actually functioning in apostolic teaching, anointing and *charisma* of the Spirit) is far more important than simply being in the line of succession. Spirit-infused apostleship should have preference over a powerless form of apostolicity. That some have confidence in their succession line alone, and claim apostolic authority solely on the basis of their valid consecration (based only upon historic apostolic succession), smacks of "blue-bloodedness." This aristocratic approach to apostolic ministry grieves God. What ultimate good is a valid consecration if a person has no verifiable anointing or significant apostolic fruit?

This reminds me of the words of John the Baptist in Luke 3:8: "*Produce fruit in keeping with repentance. And do not begin to say to yourselves, "We have Abraham as our father." For I tell you that out of these stones God can raise up children for Abraham.*'" In this case, John the Baptist required fruit over bloodline. Past and present cases of bishops who have departed from the biblical faith and practice serve to remind us that this office is truly valid only if it is practiced in a scriptural pattern.

A strong argument can be made biblically for God Himself bypassing an established order, even an order that He has ordained. Consider Eldad's and Medad's prophecies while in the camp instead of with the other elders,[66] or the man who drove out demons even though he was not an officially sanctioned disciple.[67] Each of these circumstances, one from the Old Testament and one from the New Testament, demonstrate that God can and does use individuals outside of a given normality or order. Interestingly, in both cases, it was the God-fearing men already established in the previously given divine order, not God Himself, who wanted to prevent those who were "outside" from being used of God. Not much has changed on the human side of this issue since the time of Moses. We are still quite uncomfortable whenever God changes the established order, even for a moment.

Both Moses and Jesus gave us a model for behavior toward those we perceive as "out of order." We must acknowledge God in all things that He does. Yet, even though Moses and Jesus both granted validity to those who were outside of the established order, they did not disapprove that order. They simply pointed out that God can act outside our humanly understood boundaries. Therefore, we must be wise and gracious in our approach to these things while upholding accountability as a vital component of ministry. Perhaps this is another example of God ordaining a holy tension between two distinct but inseparable patterns of leadership, as discussed earlier.

Apostolic succession, which sustains both credibility and accountability, is clearly useful. The apostle Paul was distinctly called and anointed by God, having received the apostolic blessing through the laying on of hands by the presbytery at Antioch.[68] Still, he found it needful to be personally known and affirmed by the principal apostle in Jerusalem.[69] Again,

---

66. Numbers 11:24-30.
67. Luke 9:49-50.
68. Acts 13:1-3.
69. Galatians 1:18.

years later, when his ministry focus shifted entirely to the Gentiles, he went back to Jerusalem for official confirmation of his ministry.[70] There is no positive New Testament example of apostles or others in ministry declaring themselves "valid ministers" and launching out on their own without being in direct fellowship with the apostles or their appointed protégés. Those such as Diotrephes who tried to operate independently were held in disdain.[71]

It is far better then to have both the apostolic tradition (biblical orthodoxy and supernatural apostolic ministry expression) and apostolic succession (historical continuity of apostolic authority). To have one without the other is an incomplete expression of the primitive church and, perhaps, a hindrance to the fulfillment of the church's work today.

If the consecration and functional ministry of bishops is relevant for today and has a historic and contemporary potential to be a primary form of visible unity in the church, then this tradition and succession of apostolic ministry must go forward into the various expressions of His body. Perhaps the charismatic/Pentecostal branches of the church can help restore more of a biblical "signs of an apostle model"[72] and the evangelical branches can help restore more of a biblical "teaching and evangelism-centered model"[73] that would complement and balance the apostolic succession that has been held by and preserved by the historically liturgical branches of the church. As has always been true, the people of God today need to have a prophetic leadership structure blended with a strategic leadership structure.

Jesus established a new order of priesthood after the *"order of Melchizedek."*[74] In this case, the greater included the lesser. In other words, what Jesus brought in His new order of priesthood

---

70. Galatians 2:1-10.
71. 3 John 9-10.
72. 2 Corinthians 12:12; Acts 2:42-43.
73. Acts 4:2.
74. Hebrews 7:11-12.

was superior to that which had been. But the new order did not exclude what had gone before; it simply made it better. We can draw several conclusions from this. First, it is apparent that one order may need to be replaced by another. Secondly, a replacement doesn't have to exclude, but it can include and improve that which preceded it. Finally, we can use this change of order of priesthood from Aaron to Melchizedek as a model for improvement of the historical pastoral offices to a modern-day expression.

Simply stated, there is much to learn from, esteem and bring forward from the past. We do not have to grope around or experiment without knowledge as we practice church order today. Perhaps a new order is coming, but it will probably strongly resemble what has been, even while being completely unique and fresh.

Key Discussion Points:

1. Bishops as examples for all Christians.
2. Ten roles of bishops/Christian leaders in the contemporary church.
3. Function over form.

Questions:

1. Do you agree that our leaders should be held to higher standards?
2. How would biblically and historically appointed apostolic leaders such as bishops help the church to finish the task?
3. Would functional bishops as described by the author help the current state of the church or just add another layer of distraction or dissent?

Chapter Nine

—∞∞∞—

Road Map to the Finish Line

M y food,' said Jesus, 'is to do the will of him who sent me and to finish his work.'"[1] Jesus was always clear about what He was accomplishing during His time on earth. He knew that the finish line for His earthly ministry was the cross. He could not be dissuaded from it since "'*it was for this very reason*'"[2] He had come to earth.

What then is the finish line for the church? The Great Commission is our primary target. The Great Commandment is our pattern of behavior toward God and one another, and our motivation toward those who are still lost. To be truly apostolic, fulfilling Christ's command to "'*make disciples of all nations*,'" we must be truly catholic in our attitude and practice.

Is organizational connection required for the entire church to be visibly connected? In other words, is it necessary for the church to be reunited in some form of agreed-upon organizational structure, or can its unity be organic in nature, making it

---

1. John 4:34.
2. John 12:27.

more like an ever-changing living organism that has many parts but one body? I maintain that it is possible to have one DNA but many distinct yet inseparable parts. To cultivate a living structure such as this, we must depend not only on what the church has historically experienced, but also on that which is new and freshly reconfigured. Courage and innovation will need to be balanced with intentionality and prudence.

The Ancient Made New

Consider Jesus' comment on how we can benefit from both the anciently proven and the contemporarily fashioned: *"'Therefore every teacher of the law who has been instructed about the kingdom of heaven is like the owner of a house who brings out of his storeroom new treasures as well as old.'"*[3] In His own words, Jesus gives us a potential model for moving the church forward to the finish line. We, too, must bring out *"new treasures as well as old."*

Is it possible to be old and new at the same time? Science can help us here. Let us consider the "fractal." A brief conversation with Winkey Pratney[4] some years ago, a delightful experience indeed, opened the world of fractals to me. As we enthusiastically discussed how the church could be both historical and brand new at the same time, he remarked, "Yes, the church is like a fractal." As defined in *Merriam-Webster's Collegiate Dictionary*[5] a fractal is "any of various extremely irregular curves or shapes for which any suitably chosen part is similar in shape to a given larger or smaller part when magnified or reduced to the same size." This word describes a similarity of shapes of different objects, without those objects being exactly the same, coming forth in random action.

---

3. Matthew 13:52.
4. Winkey Pratney is a noted author and speaker.
5. *Merriam-Webster's Collegiate Dictionary*, Tenth Edition, 1995, published by Merriam-Webster Incorporated.

Scientists, especially in the world of scientific mathematics, have long struggled to understand how random events fit into an otherwise linear world, and how certain objects, though random in nature, seem to have order and similarity even though their exact form cannot be predicted. Chaos Theory is the study of random events or objects that appear to develop in an orderly manner. These random events or objects never exactly repeat, and cannot be predicted by preceding events, yet the new events and objects appear with substantial similarity that seems to follow a pattern. In other words, there is order within chaos.

Snowflakes, for instance, are fractals—substantially similar to one another, but never precisely repeated. Clouds, too, are fractals. Every cloud is unique; its precise duplicate has never existed and never will. Yet, when you see a cloud, you know immediately what it is. When we view a cloud, we recognize it as a cloud, though we are actually seeing this distinct cloud for the very first time.

How can we recognize so effortlessly what we have never seen before? The unique shapes and curves in the cloud's whole or in its parts are clearly cloud-like. Though it is not an exact copy of any cloud we have formerly seen, we can still recognize it as a cloud by its substantial similarity to all other clouds. Whether it is large or small, whether we are looking at the whole cloud or just a small part of it, we can easily distinguish it as a cloud. Like snowflakes, each cloud is absolutely unique. What has been is again, yet unique. It is both old and new simultaneously. It has the shape of that which has been, but it is presented in a brand-new expression. Therefore, something can be both similar to the past, and completely new and fresh at the same time.

The church could be seen as a fractal in its nature, with easily recognized shapes that we first see in the church in the wilderness and later, more clearly, in the New Testament church. The church today is both ancient and contemporary simultaneously. Whatever the future may hold for the church, it will be easily recognizable, yet fresh and new. The same basic shapes will be evident, but perhaps put together in a form never before seen. It is almost as if there is a DNA within the church so that no matter how many times the church changes, it stays substantially the same.

Another scientific principle, called "Determinism," may help us understand what we are up against in our mindset regarding the church. "Determinism is the belief that every action is the result of preceding actions. It began as a philosophical belief in Greece thousands of years ago and was introduced into science around A.D. 1500 with the idea that cause and effect rules govern science."[6] The effect of deterministic thinking is to assume that every current event is directly determined by what preceded it.

To a significant degree, current thought about church structure is based on a form of determinism. For example, because they are deterministic in their view, many believe that the New Testament church, which they consider to be presented in a completed model, can be repeated only in its precise form. In other words, according to this line of thinking, the church of today can be accurately predicted from what has preceded it because it will be determined by what has happened previously. Traditionalists, on the other hand, would not lock in the future of the church to the pattern of the New Testament exclusively; rather, they would include a pattern developed during the Patristic period and even later. The consequence of these kinds of assumptions is that we become locked into "deterministic thinking," assuming that everything that will ever be has already been, and by having already existed, has predetermined the future. In other words, what has been should not or cannot be changed.

Unfortunately, most people tend to extrapolate whatever is current along a straight line into the future. This method of reasoning is called "linear thinking," and assumes that whatever

---

6. From a paper written by Jonathan Mendelson and Elana Blumenthal titled "Chaos Theory and Fractals."

system we have today will continue, essentially unchanged, as the pattern for the future. Linear thinking, combined with deterministic thinking, essentially guarantees that no change, even if needed, will ever be easily accepted. In fact, change may even be violently resisted.

My position, as developed in an earlier chapter, is that a simple form of church structure is presented in the New Testament, but the completed form has yet to be fully revealed. What has been, in this case, does not completely determine what will be.

Therefore, as we approach the church of the end times, we must break from deterministic and linear thinking and look for new ways to preserve the New Testament and historical shape of the church while allowing for new forms to emerge. These new forms will, of course, need to be constantly scrutinized by comparison to scriptural and historical witness. The question remains: Can the church of today be both old and new? Can the transcendent, non-changing elements of the church be fully manifest within an immanent, current model that has never before existed in its precise form? I believe that it can and must.

The development of the New Testament church actually looks a little chaotic as we study its progress, yet we know that God was working according to His plan and within His divine order. As the church has marched through history, seemingly random events have shaken it, reformed it and shaped it. While these events seem random, even chaotic from an earthly perspective, God is at work within them. They are not random at all. They are divinely managed milestones that are leading us to our ultimate future. "The church can be rightly understood only in an eschatological perspective. Whenever we seek to define it simply in terms of what it is, we go astray.... The church is not merely a historical reality but also an eschatological one."[7]

---

7. Lesslie Newbigin, *The Household of God*, Paternoster Press, London, first published 1953 (SCM Press Ltd.), reprinted 1998, p. 181.

A New Reformation

Is a new reformation about to occur? I submit that it already has begun. In fact, I propose that the modern convergence of the church toward unity for completion of the Great Commission began somewhere around the time of the birth of Methodism and caught fire in the middle 1800s during the holiness movement. Most of the new developments in the church at large to this point in history brought more division, but the holiness movement crossed over most of the lines of division at that time. It became the springboard for the modern Pentecostal movement (early 1900s) and, ultimately, the charismatic movement, which has caused more blurring of divisional lines than any event in church history. Vinson Synan states: "Without intending to do so, the Pentecostal/Charismatic Movement became the largest and most dynamic grassroots ecumenical force in the Christian world in the last decades of the 20th century."[8] He continues: "In fact, Pentecostals had barely begun talking to one another when the Charismatic Movement brought into the picture a whole new generation of Spirit-filled Christians in the mainline churches. Before Pentecostals could adjust to the fact that mainline Protestants were speaking in tongues, the Catholic Charismatic renewal began and brought with it a whole new perplexing set of ecumenical problems." These movements have created connections and produced similarities of piety and practice across the spectrum of the church. From the time they began, church leaders and laypeople alike have had to confront their meaning and make almost constant adjustments to their existence—in simple terms, reformation.

Dr. C. Peter Wagner refers to a "New Apostolic Reformation."[9] While I am still digesting some of his conclusions, I

---

8. Vinson Synan, *The Century of the Holy Spirit: 100 Years of Pentecostal and Charistmaic Renewal, 1901-2001,* Thomas Nelson Inc., Nashville, Tennessee, 2001, p. 361.
9. C. Peter Wagner, *The New Apostolic Churches,* Regal Books, Ventura, California, 1998, p. 19.

applaud his insight and nomenclature as he seeks to define what is occurring in many church movements around the world.

Like the former Reformation, this new reformation of the church has been gradually developing and growing. Of course, the only true reformation and resulting lasting unity in the church will not be produced by man's efforts but by the Spirit of God for the purpose of bringing in the final harvest. May He grant us the grace to recognize, cooperate with and champion these changes.

A Model for Christian Unity and Cooperation

The first seven Ecumenical Councils of the church were certainly pivotal in shaping the church. Are there more recent models of bishops gathering to reform and shape the church? And could any of the more recent models be of value?

Many, of course, would point to a modern movement of cooperation for world evangelization that began to take shape in 1910 and produced a historic conference held in Jerusalem in 1928. This was followed by pivotal events in Lausanne, Switzerland (1927), Edinburgh, Scotland (1937) and Berlin, Ohio (1957). The concept of a World Council for the Church was conceived in 1938, and the council was finally fully organized in Amsterdam in 1948. The combining of many ecumenical organizations from a wide variety of segments of the church into the World Council of Churches in 1950 was seen as a major step toward visible Christian unity for the sake of the Great Commission, but it quickly fell out of favor with more conservative segments of the church because of its perceived liberal political leanings. Vatican II (1962-1965) would obviously be considered a watershed moment for the more than one billion Roman Catholics in the world, but it also had consequences for the Protestant world. The General Conference on Charismatic Renewal in Kansas City in 1977 and the Congress on the Holy Spirit and World Evangelization held in New Orleans in 1987 were significant gatherings of a broad range of Christian leaders that spawned other congresses (Indianapolis in 1990, Orlando in 1995 and St. Louis in 2000) that fostered unity focused on the fulfillment of the Great Commission. Many other notable gatherings have occurred throughout the world, particularly the modern Lausanne Movement.[10] But again, those are not universal church councils in the tradition of the first apostolic council[11] and the subsequent Ecumenical Councils of the first seven centuries, which were universally considered "authoritative." These aforementioned modern congresses were momentous in that they occurred at all, but they held little recognized authority within the church at large, beyond the events themselves.

The lack of widely recognized authority that is acceptable to the three primary streams of the church is a central issue that ultimately must be addressed if the church is to move forward. Dialogue leads to understanding. But while many of the traditional denominations have representation in the ongoing dialogues, the vast majority of independent evangelicals and the fastest growing sector of Christendom, the Pentecostal/charismatic stream, have little structure for representative dialogue.

Notwithstanding the current condition of the Episcopal Church U.S.A., a potential pathway to unity was forged more than a century ago in the Chicago-Lambeth Quadrilateral and later in the Lambeth Conference of 1888.[12] The clearest path

---

10. See Appendix IV for a more complete description of this significant movement.
11. Acts 15:1-15. This apostolically called and overseen council dealt with many of the New Testament controversies surrounding the requirements for Gentile believers. The decisions were universally endorsed, and set a precedent for subsequent Ecumenical Councils.
12. The Chicago-Lambeth Quadrilateral (1886, 1888). While the Quadrilateral was adopted by the House of Bishops, it was not enacted by the House of Deputies, but rather incorporated in a general plan referred for study and action to a Joint Commission on Christian Reunion.

to genuine unity by deferring one's own preferences I have ever seen is found in this magnificent statement from the Quadrilateral: "That in all things of human ordering or human choice, relating to modes of worship and discipline, or to traditional customs, this church is ready in the spirit of love and humility to forego all preferences of her own." These gatherings of bishops of the Protestant Episcopal Church (The U.S. Province of the worldwide Anglican Communion) produced a simple outline for conceivably bringing greater visible unity among the divergent streams of the church. Sadly, this tremendous opportunity for greater unity in the whole church was ratified twice by the House of Bishops, but was ultimately rejected by the House of Deputies and never ratified, though it does remain an important inclusion in the Prayer Book of the Episcopal Church.[13]

Selected portions[14] of the Chicago-Lambeth Quadrilateral (1886 and 1888) are as follows: "Christian unity can only be restored by the return of all Christian communions to the principles of unity exemplified by the undivided Catholic Church during the first ages of its existence; which principles we believe to be the substantial deposit of the Christian Faith and Order committed by Christ and His Apostles to the Church unto the end of the world, and therefore incapable of compromise or surrender by those who have been ordained to be its steward and trustees for the common and equal benefit of all men.

"Furthermore, deeply grieved by the sad divisions which affect the Christian Church in our own land, we hereby declare our desire and readiness, so soon as there shall be any authorized response to this Declaration, to enter into brotherly conference with all or any Christian Bodies seeking restoration of the organic unity of the Church, with a view to the earnest study of the conditions under which so priceless a blessing might happily be brought to pass.

---

13. The Book of Common Prayer, Church Hymnal Corporation, New York.
14. See Appendix III for a complete version of both the 1886 and 1888 texts of the Chicago-Lambeth Quadrilateral.

"In the opinion of this conference, the following Articles supply a basis on which approach may be by God's blessing made toward Home Reunion:

(A) The Holy Scriptures of the Old and New Testaments, as 'containing all things necessary for salvation,' and as being the rule and ultimate standard of faith.
(B) The Apostles' Creed, as the Baptismal Symbol; and the Nicene Creed, as the sufficient statement of Christian faith.
(C) The two Sacraments ordained by Christ Himself—Baptism and the Supper of the Lord—maintained with unfailing use of Christ's words of Institution, and of the elements ordained by Him.
(D) The Historic Episcopate, locally adapted in the methods of its administration to the varying needs of the nations and peoples called of God into the Unity of His Church."

Whether or not this particular outline for visible unity will work, one thing is sure, we must not give up on Jesus' prayer for us to be one. Could we use the Chicago-Lambeth Quadrilateral as it is, modify it or come up with something better? It is sad that such a beautiful and thoughtful statement produced by the bishops of the Episcopal Church so long ago was rejected and never implemented as a tool of unity. To strengthen the need for additional clarity of orthodoxy, the Lausanne Covenant[15] may serve to undergird the use of the Quadrilateral as a model for organic unity.

The general condition of many of the traditional denominations today makes this seem even more impossible. We cannot, however, surrender the possibility of organic unity to the difficulties of present circumstances in the global church.

---

15. See Appendix V.

The Anointing

We must stand firm in faith that Jesus' prayer for unity and His command to reach every nation will both be fulfilled in our lifetime. Can any real change occur without the anointing of the Holy Spirit? Consider the admonition of the apostle Paul in 2 Corinthians 1:21-22: *"Now it is God who makes both us and you stand firm in Christ. He anointed us, set his seal of ownership on us, and put his Spirit in our hearts as a deposit, guaranteeing what is to come."* According to Paul, it is the Spirit of God who makes us stand firm. It is the Spirit of God who anoints us. It is the Spirit of God who seals and guarantees what is to come. We must learn to walk in cadence with the Holy Spirit to meet the challenges set before us.

Although every branch of the church believes in the continuing role of the Spirit of God in the affairs of the church, many simply assign His role to one of mystery and distance from the daily affairs of man. We must move from purely intellectual acknowledgment and assent to actually yielding to the voice of God's Spirit, both personally and institutionally. Christian leaders not only must possess a theology of the Holy Spirit, but must have personal experience with and maintain an open ear to His daily promptings. This point is beautifully made by Dr. Gordon Fee in the introduction of his book *God's Empowering Presence*: "For some, a book on the Spirit as 'theology' is the kiss of death; and in many ways, I am in that camp. But we lack a better word; and in the final analysis, the health of the contemporary church necessitates that its theology of the Spirit and its experience of the Spirit correspond more closely."[16] Not only the *health* of the contemporary church, but the *mission* of the contemporary church is dependent upon a new level of correspondence between what we *believe* and what we actually *experience*.

---

16. Gordon D. Fee, *God's Empowering Presence*, Hendrickson Publishers, Inc., Peabody, Massachusetts, 1994, p. 2.

The necessity of guidance and empowerment from the Holy Spirit in matters of church unity and the Great Commission cannot be overstated. The church must be *dressed for battle* in these last days and surrendered to God's purpose; but, above all, we must be anointed by the Holy Spirit or all of our efforts will be for naught. God instructed Moses to prepare Aaron and his sons for ministry with these words: *"After you put these clothes on your brother Aaron and his sons, anoint and ordain them. Consecrate them so they may serve me as priests."*[17] I notice that the *anointing* preceded their *consecration* to ministry. To be consecrated means "to be dedicated to a sacred purpose."[18] It is impossible for us to achieve absolute, unmitigated and unwavering *consecration* to the sacred purpose of unity in the church for the completion of the Great Commission without the *anointing* and constant superintendence of the Holy Spirit. Jesus, the fountainhead of our faith and ministry, pointed to the priority of the anointing when He declared: *"'The Spirit of the LORD is on me, because he has anointed me to preach good news to the poor. He has sent me to proclaim freedom for the prisoners and recovery of sight for the blind, to release the oppressed, to proclaim the year of the LORD's favor.'"*[19] The success of His earthly ministry was dependent upon the anointing of the Spirit, as ours is.

God has preserved throughout the ages the promise of the catholicity of the church (the unity of the church) and the apostolicity of the church (the tradition and succession of the apostles) that they may now assist this generation to fulfill His will and command. An accurate understanding of apostolic succession and tradition requires recognizing that God has been divinely present with and continually working through His church throughout the ages. The anointing and blessing placed upon Peter and all the early apostles has an unbroken

---

17. Exodus 28:41.
18. *Merriam-Webster's Collegiate Dictionary*, Tenth Edition, 1995, published by Merriam-Webster Incorporated.
19. Luke 4:18-19.

stream of consistency from the founding of the church to the present. Though this unbroken stream has often been ignored, misunderstood or practically invisible, God has preserved it for His own purposes. This continuity can be traced in two separate but equally important ways: apostolic tradition and apostolic succession.

The development of church structure was a process. It has continued to emerge throughout history. We must be cautious in hastily adopting a pattern and confidently declaring it as the universally right one because the development of the end-time church for which Christ is coming is still an awaited promise.

It is time to have a renewed vision of what the church can be, *must* and *will* be. We can actually get an idea of where we are going by careful consideration of what is now occurring. This approach is addressed by Dr. Rick Warren: "Most people think of 'vision' as the ability to see the future. But in today's rapidly changing world, vision is also the ability to accurately assess current changes and take advantage of them. Vision is being alert to opportunities."[20] The need for alertness is greater than ever. With the advent of modern technology and the increased communications and travel opportunities that technology provides, along with the internationalization of the church as Christian population centers shift, the vision and action of the church is changing rapidly. Our sovereign King, precisely because He is sovereign, is moving in the earth in unprecedented ways without our permission and, in many cases, without our acknowledgment or intentional cooperation. God has thrown down the gauntlet by invoking unity and clarity of focus on the remaining task throughout the streams of the church on an unparalleled worldwide scale. How shall we as the people of God—the one holy catholic and apostolic church of the Firstborn—respond to heaven's overtures to work together to finish the task? We must accept heaven's challenge

---

20. Rick Warren, *The Purpose Driven Church*, Zondervan Corporation, Grand Rapids, Michigan, 1995, p. 28.

and pick up the gauntlet. Richard Foster asserts: "Right now we remain largely a scattered people. This has been the condition of the Church of Jesus Christ for a good many years. But a new thing is coming. God is gathering His people once again. Creating of them an all-inclusive community of loving persons with Jesus Christ as the community's prime sustained and most glorious inhabitant. This community is breaking forth in multiplied ways in various forms."[21]

As the church continues to enlarge and expand throughout the earth, we will confront new challenges and opportunities. Old structures will serve us well, but only as they are adapted to present needs and applied with the might and guidance of the Holy Spirit. The church is growing faster than at any time in history, and all the while, God is bringing unity and strategic cooperation to His body in the earth in an unprecedented way. We are already well along into a modern-day reformation. The current worldwide growth of the church and the doctrinal and cooperative demands that this rapid expansion has produced are bringing fresh interest and need for the restoration of the apostolic offices in branches of the church that have had little historical interest in bishops. These bishops, along with all clergy and leaders, must work diligently to foster true unity and cooperation at every stratum of the church, especially on the local level.

We must be willing to stretch our thinking and our structures to accommodate this time of new beginnings. We cannot allow ignorance, fear or shame to keep us from finishing the work in the earth that we may enjoy the reward of eternity.

While God could have chosen a different path to finish His work on the earth, He did not. He has chosen His church, the one holy catholic and apostolic church, to be His witness in the earth. Now it is our mission, desire and duty to please our Supreme Commander.

---

21. Richard J. Foster, *Streams of Living Water*, HarperCollins Publishers, San Francisco, 1998, p. 273.

I recently participated in a dedication service for a newly built synagogue near our church. As I prepared to do a reading and offer prayer, I noticed a banner near the podium written in Hebrew. I asked Rabbi Eliezer Ben-Yehuda[22] for a translation of the words. They were simple but searing: "KNOW BEFORE WHOM YOU STAND." When standing before God, there must be acknowledgement of His sovereign will and power. As we stand before God, how can we disregard Jesus' prayer for unity or His command to take the Gospel of the kingdom to every tribe, people, language and nation? Knowing before whom we stand means that we must abandon half-hearted, lethargic attempts to unite under the banner of Christ and, for the sake of His command, that we passionately pursue His stated will that as "one" we finish our earthly work!

Though we may attempt to fulfill His will without His empowerment, our only hope for success is Him. St. Augustine said it so succinctly:

Without God, we cannot.
Without us, He will not.

If we are to even consider laying down our own preferences to come together in visible unity for the sake of finishing the task that Christ has directly commissioned, we must first embrace the cross of Christ. It is only in "taking up"[23] the cross that we will experience the needed humility and selflessness to actually embrace one another. The cross is our central message, our peace with God and one another, and our pathway to undivided attention to God's purpose on the earth. As we each individually, and as branches and streams of the church, attempt to flow into one river, we will succeed only as we live

---

22. Rabbi Eliezer Ben-Yehuda is the spiritual leader of the Beth El Synagogue in Ponte Vedra Beach, Florida. He bears the name of his grandfather, who is credited with pioneering the restoration of the modern Hebrew language as a spoken language, particularly in Palestine (modern-day Israel).
23. Matthew 10:38.

under the shadow of the cross. Death to self, to personal preferences and to humanly devised plans will result in the release of life and light to the world around us.

His "one holy catholic and apostolic church" is truly a church for all ages, having a rich past, a dynamic present and a glorious future. Is there any truth to the proposition that God has designed the different streams of the church to emphasize and express unique elements of His nature as Father, Son and Holy Spirit? If so, we should remember that while each Person of the Trinity is *distinct*, there is no *distance* between them. So even though we may have legitimate distinctions from one another, it is now time to remove any distance between the streams so that we may flow together freely.

In closing, I offer two passages from Scripture. The first has become my personal marching orders:

Isaiah 54:2-5: "'*Enlarge the place of your tent, stretch your tent curtains wide, do not hold back; lengthen your cords, strengthen your stakes. For you will spread out to the right and to the left; your descendents will dispossess nations and settle in their desolate cities. Do not be afraid; you will not suffer shame. Do not fear disgrace; you will not be humiliated. You will forget the shame of your youth and remember no more the reproach of your widowhood. For your Maker is your husband—the* LORD *Almighty is his name—the Holy One of Israel is your Redeemer; he is called the God of all the earth.*'"

The church is challenged to push forward at any cost. We cannot afford a small vision or limited belief of what God can do in and through His church. We will forget past failures and reproach. We will accomplish the earthy work of the church. We will.

The second closing passage I offer contains the prayer of Jesus for unity in His church. This is a prayer for unity with purpose. Divinely granted unity will empower us to finish the task of preaching the Gospel and making disciples in every nation. His prayer is still resounding in the heavenlies until that glorious day in which it comes to pass. May this become our prevailing prayer and daily pursuit:

John 17:20-23: *"My prayer is not for them alone. I pray also for those who will believe in me through their message, that all of them may be one, Father, just as you are in me and I am in you. May they also be in us so that the world may believe that you have sent me. I have given them the glory that you gave me, that they may be one as we are one: I in them and you in me. May they be brought to complete unity to let the world know that you sent me and have loved them even as you have loved me."*

The church in all of its magnificent diversity is surging forward, gaining strength as its many streams flow together, until all of our differences will be lost in the din of praise of the Lamb...the *sound of rushing waters.*

Key Discussion Points:

1. The ancient made new.
2. The restoration of universally recognized church councils.
3. A pathway to unity—The Chicago-Lambeth Quadrilateral.
4. Guidance and empowerment from the Holy Spirit to finish the task.

Questions:

1. Is there a finish line for the church on earth and what is it?
2. Can the church be faithful to its basic ancient elements and remain current with contemporary or future needs? If so, describe how this might be done.
3. In your opinion, does the Chicago-Lambeth Quadrilateral provide a sufficient model for unity in the church? Describe its strengths and weaknesses.
4. In addition to those presented by the author, are there other models for unity from which we can learn?

Appendix I

━━━━━━ ❦ ━━━━━━

Additional Information on the Author's Journey

Part of my conflict in writing this book has been an innate desire to maintain the focus on "the main thing": organic unity for the completion of the Great Commission. While my personal testimony and background are central to my own journey, they may not be important to the reader's. In an attempt to provide what may be helpful to some without bogging down the central message of the book, I have left some of the details of my life to this appendix. I hope it is helpful.

The Lord's path for my life has taken me through a maze of ministry experiences, including the local Southern Baptist Church where I was first licensed to preach, the Christian Church-Church of Christ where I was initially ordained, independent charismatic churches, the Episcopal Church, classical Pentecostal churches and finally, to convergence.

In June 1973, Sharon and I were married in Jacksonville, Florida, after attending the same high school and dating from age 16. I was licensed a Baptist minister at age 18 (August 1973) at Arlington Baptist Church. During that period, I served as the leader of the high school youth group and co-founded

"Crossroads," a coffeehouse ministry to hippies and bikers in a storefront. We had our first son, Barry.

In January 1975, at age 19, I became the youth pastor, school bus driver and part-time janitor of Beaches Chapel Christian Church, Church of Christ. Sharon and I simultaneously operated a live-in rehabilitation ministry with approximately 50 people living in our facilities. We formed Spirit of Life Ministries and opened another storefront coffeehouse outreach ministry at the Jacksonville Beach boardwalk.

In January of 1976, at age 20, I was sanctioned and supported as a "home missionary" by Beaches Chapel. In November 1976, we moved Spirit of Life Ministries, our outreach and rehabilitation work, to the inner city of Jacksonville. I worked closely with a United Methodist pastor and a Presbyterian pastor while planting Springfield Community Church and continuing our "Christian Community" rehabilitation and Christian discipleship ministry. We housed as many as 120 families and singles in our community facilities. We had our second son, Ben.

In 1978, at age 23, I was ordained by Beaches Chapel Christian Church. In June of that year, I was received as a "visiting clergy" by St. Peter's Episcopal Church to serve as youth pastor and worship leader. Our daughter, Bethany, was born, and later, our son Brian.

In June 1981, at age 26, we founded Calvary International. In January 1982, at age 27, we moved to San Jose, Costa Rica, Central America to attend language school and begin our work as missionaries with Las Iglesias Evangelicas Nacionales de Costa Rica.

In September 1983, at age 28, we teamed up with five other missionaries and nationals to co-found Cristo Al Mundo, a Bible training center in the heart of downtown San Jose.

In June 1985, at age 30, we moved as a team with four other missionary families to Quito, Ecuador, South America, to co-found Cristo Al Mundo.

In August 1986, at age 31, we moved back to Jacksonville to strengthen our ministry headquarters and to co-found Christ to the World Bible Training Center.

In January 1992, we began Christ the Redeemer Church in Ponte Vedra Beach, Florida. I simultaneously functioned as the president of Calvary International and as the senior pastor of Christ the Redeemer Church until July 2000, at which time Jerry Williamson was selected to the presidency of Calvary International. I am now serving Calvary International as a board member and as president emeritus.

In 1999, I was consecrated into historical apostolic succession as a bishop by the laying on of hands of three duly authorized bishops.

During most of my 19-year tenure as president of Calvary International, I also served as the chairman of the Agency Services Committee, which provided oversight of services to its more than one hundred member agencies and institutions, and on the board of trustees of AIMS (Accelerating International Mission Strategies), under the leadership of its president and founder, Dr. Howard Foltz. This position was a unique place for personal growth, fellowship and association with great mission leaders from around the globe. Innumerable influences impacted my personal life and my public ministry through my association with AIMS, not the least of which was the dogged determination of Dr. Foltz to challenge the church to finish the task by reaching the least-reached peoples of the earth.

It has also been my privilege since 1996 to serve as chairman of the board of Teen Mania, one of the largest and most effective youth ministries in the world, led by its president and founder, Ron Luce. This involvement has combined three of my lifelong passions—working with young people, cross-cultural ministry and cross-denominational ministry—along with the privilege of working with the executive staff, the exceptional company of board members and, especially, Ron and Katie Luce, two of the finest and most effective Christians that I have ever known.

All of this has been by the grace and destiny of God. These involvements, along with many others not mentioned, have provided personal association with some of the greatest men and women of God in this generation. There are simply too many to mention. I have done nothing to deserve the opportunities that God has offered.

The Lord Himself has caused me to walk in many divergent paths so that I might have a personal appreciation for different age groups, cultures, languages, socioeconomic levels and doctrinal emphases. In recent years, this diversity of background and experiences has led me to these conclusions:

- I am, first and foremost, a Great Commission Christian, being dedicated to its fulfillment in our generation.
- My history, beliefs and ministry style are a blend of evangelical/fundamentalism, charismatic/Pentecostalism and liturgical/sacramentalism.
- This diversity in my life and ministry, while being unplanned on my part, was planned and ordained by God. Frankly, it has been both a blessing and a source of discomfort, since it has provided wonderful texture and value to my own life, but has made it difficult to be an easy fit into any one stream of the church.
- I have always had an extraordinary love and respect for the whole church in all its glorious theological, racial, cultural, missional and symbolic diversity.

Christ the Redeemer Church

In 1989, while I was still president of Calvary International and we were preparing to enter into extensive ministry in the Soviet Union, God began to move deeply within me to plant a convergence church where we lived in Ponte Vedra Beach, a community in the Jacksonville, Florida, metro area. Our area was (and still is) one of the fastest growing in our state, but had relatively few churches. I had a vision of a church that would be intentionally evangelical, sacramental and charismatic in its worship style and mission. We prayed over this decision for three years. With some concern for how we could do a successful church plant with such a unique style of worship while still overseeing Calvary International and traveling regularly to the Soviet Union and beyond, we began with four families in our living room in January 1992.

From those meager beginnings, Christ the Redeemer has grown to be a strong local church with a vision of spiritual transformation for our city, nation and world. At the time of this writing, some 13 years later, attendance at our principal weekend services has grown to approximately one thousand and our membership to approximately sixteen hundred. We have planted another "Christ the Redeemer Church" on Amelia Island, about 45 miles to our north, another in St. Augustine to our south, and are training leaders to plant additional congregations.

Every local church has distinguishing characteristics that express the priorities of its mission. These distinctives act as navigational points by which we can appraise whether or not we are on course. Distinctives may change over time, but only through a slow process as a ministry adjusts to prevailing needs and divine direction that come from time to time. Our distinctives as a congregation and family of churches are as follows:

- **A full expression of the historical and contemporary streams of the church where the sacramental, evangelical and charismatic converge.** 1 Corinthians 12:4-6: *"There are different kinds of gifts, but the same Spirit. There are different kinds of service, but the same LORD. There are different kinds of working, but the same God works all of them in all men."*
- **An unflinching resolve to recognize and promote the priesthood of all believers.** Ephesians 2:10: *"For we are God's workmanship, created in Christ Jesus to do good works, which God prepared in advance for us to do."*
- **A vigorous devotion to train a generation of young people to fulfill their God-given destiny.** Psalm 78:4: *"We will tell the next generation the praiseworthy deeds of the LORD, his power, and the wonders he has done."*

- An absolute dedication to the fulfillment of the Great Commission in this generation. Matthew 28:19-20: *"'Therefore go and make disciples of all nations, baptizing them in the name of the Father and of the Son and of the Holy Spirit, and teaching them to obey everything I have commanded you. And surely I will be with you always, to the very end of the age.'"*
- A determined commitment to minister to the sick, the broken and the needy, and to help mend human divisions. Luke 4:18: *"'The Spirit of the LORD is on me, because he has anointed me to preach good news to the poor. He has sent me to proclaim freedom for the prisoners and recovery of sight for the blind, to release the oppressed.'"*

The International Communion of Christian Churches

On February 10, 1999, I was consecrated a bishop with valid orders into historic apostolic succession, after almost two years of examination and specified study. I was commissioned by my consecrating bishops, the Most Rev. Wayne Boosahda, the Right Rev. Michael Owen and the Right Rev. Van Gayton, to form a new communion of churches with convergence as its center—the International Communion of Christian Churches.[1] We simultaneously established intercommunion relationships with the Communion of Evangelical Episcopal Churches and later, the International Community of Christian Churches. In the spirit of the Chicago-Lambeth Quadrilateral,[2] we have

---

1. The style of convergence that our provincial diocese has chosen has no specific preference in sacramentalism, evangelicalism or Pentecostalism. Our intent is that all of the streams flow together and are regularly expressed in our worship and mission without identifying our churches or clergy within one specific primary stream.
2. The Chicago-Lambeth Quadrilateral is discussed in more detail in the final chapter of this book, and is presented by this author as a potential pathway to greater Christian unity and cooperation.

continued to form relationships with other segments of the body of Christ as opportunity arises.

A recent and significant change is the merger of the ICCC and the Province of the U.S.A. of the CEEC to form a national communion in the U.S. The name of this new national communion is the Communion of Convergence Churches USA.[3] Our mission is the apostolic empowerment of God's people for service through convergence of Scripture, Spirit and Sacrament to fulfill the Great Commandment and the Great Commission. This newly organized communion is a province of the CEEC.

As a bishop, I am under no organizational constraint to function with a specific preference of liturgy as I carry out my ministry, but I do respectfully participate in ceremony and practice as is appropriate with my liturgically centered brethren, as well as on high holy days and in special services within our own churches, diocese and communion.

My personal goal, in the meantime, is to understand and promote the historical streams of the church in a blended form of worship and mission. The church can be evangelical, stressing salvation by faith in the atoning death of Jesus Christ through personal conversion, the authority and inerrancy of the Bible, the necessity of evangelism at home and abroad, the priesthood of the believer, and the importance of Spirit-anointed preaching as contrasted with mere ritual. The church also can be sacramental, practicing the historically recognized rites that are vital to worship and have been preserved and practiced throughout the ages. We can highly value the sacraments and sacramentalism, use the primary ancient creeds, and encourage the use of a liturgy based on biblical and historic traditions along with historic ceremony and Christian symbolism. Lastly, the church can be Pentecostal, emphasizing the free expression of the gifts and person of the

---

3. The Communion of Convergence Churches, U.S.A. is the publicly used name for the Communion. The official name is the Communion of Episcopal Convergence Churches USA.

Holy Spirit, especially in expressive praise and in signs and wonders, a second experience in filling of the Holy Spirit, personal spiritual growth and holiness, and everyone's individual call to ministry.

Though I am now consecrated into apostolic succession as practiced in the historical churches, my "center" remains in an intentionally and delicately balanced convergence. I will, however, continue my own studies and embrace of historical Christianity and encourage others to do the same. I will seek out those who are moving toward this convergence of streams and encourage others to join us in this pursuit. We remain open to the yet unseen plan of God.

The journey continues.

The Primary Creeds

The Nicene Creed
We believe in one God,
  the Father, the Almighty,
  Maker of heaven and earth,
  of all that is, seen or unseen.

We believe in one Lord, Jesus Christ,
  the only Son of God,
  eternally begotten of the Father,
  God from God, Light from Light,
  true God from true God,
  begotten, not made,
  of one Being with the Father.
  Through Him all things were made.
  For us and for our salvation
    He came down from heaven:
  by the power of the Holy Spirit
    He became incarnate from the Virgin Mary,
    and was made man.
  For our sake He was crucified under Pontius Pilate;
    He suffered death and was buried.

On the third day He rose again
    in accordance with the Scriptures;
He ascended into heaven
    and is seated at the right hand of the Father.
He will come again in glory to judge the living and the dead,
    and His kingdom will have no end.

We believe in the Holy Spirit, the Lord, the giver of life,
    who proceeds from the Father (and the Son).[1]
With the Father and the Son He is worshiped and glorified.
He has spoken through the Prophets.
We believe in one holy catholic and apostolic Church.
We acknowledge one baptism for the forgiveness of sins.
We look for the resurrection of the dead,
    and the life of the world to come. Amen.

The Apostles' Creed

I believe in God, the Father almighty,
    Creator of heaven and earth.
I believe in Jesus Christ, His only Son, our Lord.
    He was conceived by the power of the Holy Spirit
        and born of the Virgin Mary.
    He suffered under Pontius Pilate,
        was crucified, died, and was buried.

---

1. The original phrase as proclaimed in A.D. 325 at the Council of Nicea was "proceeds from the Father." The phrase "and the Son" was added in A.D. 589 by a local council in Toledo, Spain. This began the "*filioque* debate." The phrase "and the Son" in Latin is the word *filioque*. The *filioque* was officially declared as the official wording of the Nicene Creed by the Roman pope (the bishop of Rome) around the same time that he ex-communicated the patriarch of Constantinople, effectively dividing the one holy catholic and apostolic church in two, east and west, in A.D. 1054. There remains a valid argument from the Orthodox Churches that Jesus Himself taught that the Holy Spirit proceeds from the Father as described in John 15:26: "'But when the Comforter is come, whom I will send unto you from the Father, even the Spirit of truth, *which proceedeth from the father,* he shall testify of me'" (KJV). However, Galatians 4:6 seems to support the Western view: "'Because you are sons, God sent the Spirit of his Son into our hearts, the Spirit who calls out, 'Abba, Father'" (NIV).

He descended to the dead.
On the third day He rose again.
He ascended into heaven,
    and is seated at the right hand of the Father.
He will come again to judge the living and the dead.
I believe in the Holy Spirit,
    the holy catholic Church,
    the communion of saints,
    the forgiveness of sins,
    the resurrection of the body,
    and the life everlasting. Amen.

Appendix III

---ooo---

Common Elements of Convergence Churches[1]

- A restored dedication to the sacraments, especially the Lord's Table.
- An identification and connection with the historical church, particularly the church of the first four centuries.
- An embrace of the historic episcopate in some expression, with an emphasis upon the restoration of the office of bishop in the apostolic and historic tradition.
- A love and embrace for the whole church and a desire to see genuine catholicity resulting in increased unity and cooperation.
- The blending of the different practices of the different streams is evident, yet each church approaches convergence from its own views and emphases.
- An interest in a harmonious mixture of structure, symbolism, biblical preaching and Spirit-led worship.
- A comprehensive commitment to the Great Commandment and the Great Commission.

---

1. This list of characteristics was originally presented in an article written by Wayne Boosahda and Randy Sly for *Twenty Centuries of Christian Worship* by Robert Webber, ed. The original list in the article presented six characteristics. I have modified and added to this list.

The Chicago-Lambeth Quadrilateral, 1886 and 1888

Adopted by the House of Bishops
Chicago, 1886

We, Bishops of the Protestant Episcopal Church in the United States of America, in Council assembled as Bishops in the Church of God, do hereby solemnly declare to all whom it may concern, and especially to our fellow-Christians of the different Communions in this land, who, in their several spheres, have contended for the religion of Christ:

1. Our earnest desire that the Savior's prayer, "That we all may be one," may, in its deepest and truest sense, be speedily fulfilled;

2. That we believe that all who have been duly baptized with water, in the name of the Father, and of the Son, and of the Holy Ghost, are members of the Holy Catholic Church;

3. That in all things of human ordering or human choice, relating to modes of worship and discipline, or to traditional customs, this Church is ready in the spirit of love and humility to forego all preferences of her own;

4. That this Church does not seek to absorb other Communions, but rather, co-operating with them on the basis of a common Faith and Order, to discountenance schism, to

heal the wounds of the Body of Christ, and to promote the charity which is the chief of Christian graces and the visible manifestation of Christ to the world.

But furthermore, we do hereby affirm that the Christian unity can only be restored by the return of all Christian communions to the principles of unity exemplified by the undivided Catholic Church during the first ages of its existence; which principles we believe to be the substantial deposit of the Christian Faith and Order committed by Christ and His Apostles to the Church unto the end of the world, and therefore incapable of compromise or surrender by those who have been ordained to be its stewards and trustees for the common and equal benefit of all men.

As inherent parts of this sacred deposit, and therefore as essential to the restoration of unity among the divided branches of Christendom, we account the following, to wit:

1. The Holy Scriptures of the Old and New Testament as the revealed Word of God.

2. The Nicene Creed as the sufficient statement of the Christian Faith.

3. The two Sacraments, Baptism and the Supper of the Lord, ministered with unfailing use of Christ's words of institution and of the elements ordained by Him.

4. The Historic Episcopate, locally adapted in the methods of its administration to the varying needs of the nations and peoples called of God into the unit of His Church.

Furthermore, deeply grieved by the sad divisions which affect the Christian Church in our own land, we hereby declare our desire and readiness, so soon as there shall be any authorized response to this Declaration, to enter into brotherly conference with all or any Christian Bodies seeking restoration of the organic unity of the Church, with a view to the earnest study of the conditions under which so priceless a blessing might happily be brought to pass.

Note: While the above form of the Quadrilateral was adopted by the House of Bishops, it was not enacted by the House of Deputies, but rather incorporated in a general plan referred for study and action to a newly created Joint Commission on Christian Reunion.

Lambeth Conference of 1888
Resolution 11

That, in the opinion of this conference, the following Articles supply a basis on which approach may be by God's blessing made toward Home Reunion:

(1) The Holy Scriptures of the Old and New Testaments, as "containing all things necessary for salvation," and as being the rule and ultimate standard of faith.

(2) The Apostles' Creed, as the Baptismal Symbol; and the Nicene Creed, as the sufficient statement of Christian faith.

(3) The two Sacraments ordained by Christ Himself—Baptism and the Supper of the Lord—maintained with unfailing use of Christ's words of Institution, and of the elements ordained by Him.

(4) The Historic Episcopate, locally adapted in the methods of its administration to the varying needs of the nations and peoples called of God into the Unity of His Church.

Appendix V

——— ∞∞ ———

The Lausanne Covenant, 1974

The Lausanne Covenant is a declaration agreed upon in Lausanne, Switzerland by more than 2,300 evangelicals during the 1974 International Congress on World Evangelization to be more intentional about world evangelization.

Introduction

We, members of the Church of Jesus Christ, from more than 150 nations, participants in the International Congress on World Evangelization at Lausanne, praise God for his great salvation and rejoice in the fellowship he has given us with himself and with each other. We are deeply stirred by what God is doing in our day, moved to penitence by our failures and challenged by the unfinished task of evangelization. We believe the Gospel is God's good news for the whole world, and we are determined by his grace to obey Christ's commission to proclaim it to all mankind and to make disciples of every nation. We desire, therefore, to affirm our faith and our resolve, and to make public our covenant.

1. THE PURPOSE OF GOD

We affirm our belief in the one eternal God, Creator and Lord of the world, Father, Son and Holy Spirit, who governs all things according to the purpose of his will. He has been calling out from the world a people for himself, and sending his people back into the world to be his servants and witnesses, for the extension of his kingdom, the building up of Christ's body, and the glory of his name. We confess with shame that we have often denied our calling and failed in our mission, by becoming conformed to the world or by withdrawing from it. Yet we rejoice that even when borne by earthen vessels the gospel is still a precious treasure. To the task of making that treasure known in the power of the Holy Spirit we desire to dedicate ourselves anew.

(Isa. 40:28; Matt. 28:19; Eph. 1:11; Acts 15:14; John 17:6,18; Eph. 4:12; 1 Cor. 5:10; Rom. 12:2; 2 Cor. 4:7)

2. THE AUTHORITY AND POWER OF THE BIBLE

We affirm the divine inspiration, truthfulness and authority of both Old and New Testament Scriptures in their entirety as the only written word of God, without error in all that it affirms, and the only infallible rule of faith and practice. We also affirm the power of God's word to accomplish his purpose of salvation. The message of the Bible is addressed to all men and women. For God's revelation in Christ and in Scripture is unchangeable. Through it the Holy Spirit still speaks today. He illumines the minds of God's people in every culture to perceive its truth freshly through their own eyes and thus discloses to the whole Church ever more of the many-colored wisdom of God.

(2 Tim. 3:16; 2 Peter 1:21; John 10:35; Isa. 55:11; 1 Cor. 1:21; Rom. 1:16; Matt. 5:17,18; Jude 3; Eph. 1:17,18; 3:10,18)

3. THE UNIQUENESS AND UNIVERSALITY OF CHRIST

We affirm that there is only one Savior and only one gospel, although there is a wide diversity of evangelistic approaches. We

recognize that every one has some knowledge of God through his general revelation in nature. But we deny that this can save, for people suppress the truth by their unrighteousness. We also reject as derogatory to Christ and the gospel every kind of syncretism and dialogue which implies that Christ speaks equally through all religions and ideologies. Jesus Christ, being himself the only God-man, who gave himself as the only ransom for sinners, is the only mediator between God and people. There is no other name by which we must be saved. All men and women are perishing because of sin, but God loves everyone, not wishing that any should perish but that all should repent. Yet those who reject Christ repudiate the joy of salvation and condemn themselves to eternal separation from God. To proclaim Jesus as "the Savior of the world" is not to affirm that all people are either automatically or ultimately saved, still less to affirm that all religions offer salvation in Christ. Rather it is to proclaim God's love for a world of sinners and to invite everyone to respond to him as Savior and Lord in wholehearted personal commitment of repentance and faith. Jesus Christ has been exalted above every other name; we long for the day when every knee shall bow to him and every tongue shall confess him Lord.
(Gal. 1:6-9; Rom. 1:18-32; 1 Tim. 2:5,6; Acts 4:12; John 3:16-19; 2 Peter 3:9; 2 Thess. 1:7-9; John 4:42; Matt. 11:28; Eph. 1:20, 21; Phil. 2:9-11)

4. THE NATURE OF EVANGELISM

To evangelize is to spread the good news that Jesus Christ died for our sins and was raised from the dead according to the Scriptures, and that as the reigning Lord he now offers the forgiveness of sins and the liberating gifts of the Spirit to all who repent and believe. Our Christian presence in the world is indispensable to evangelism, and so is that kind of dialogue whose purpose is to listen sensitively in order to understand. But evangelism itself is the proclamation of the historical, biblical Christ as Savior and Lord, with a view to persuading people to come to him personally and so be reconciled to God. In issuing the gospel invitation we have no liberty to conceal

the cost of discipleship. Jesus still calls all who should follow him to deny themselves, take up their cross, and identify themselves with his new community. The results of evangelism include obedience to Christ, incorporation into his Church and responsible service in the world.
(1 Cor. 15:3,4; Acts 2:32-39; John 20:21; 1 Cor. 1:23; 2 Cor. 4:5; 5:11,20; Luke 14:25-33; Mark 8:34; Acts 2:40,47; Mark 10:43-45)

5. CHRISTIAN SOCIAL RESPONSIBILITY

We affirm that God is both the Creator and the Judge of all men. We therefore should share his concern for justice and reconciliation throughout human society and for the liberation of men and women from every kind of oppression. Because men and women are made in the image of God, every person, regardless of race, religion, color, culture, class, sex or age, has an intrinsic dignity because of which he or she should be respected and served, not exploited. Here too we express penitence both for our neglect and for having sometimes regarded evangelism and social concern as mutually exclusive. Although reconciliation with other people is not reconciliation with God, nor is social action evangelism, nor is political liberation salvation, nevertheless we affirm that evangelism and sociopolitical involvement are both part of our Christian duty. For both are necessary expressions of our doctrines of God and man, our love for our neighbor and our obedience to Jesus Christ. The message of salvation implies also a message of judgment upon every form of alienation, oppression and discrimination, and we should not be afraid to denounce evil and injustice wherever they exist. When people receive Christ they are born again into his kingdom and must seek not only to exhibit but also to spread its righteousness in the midst of an unrighteous world. The salvation we claim should be transforming us in the totality of our personal and social responsibilities. Faith without works is dead.
(Acts 17:26,31; Gen. 18:25; Isa. 1:17; Ps. 45:7; Gen. 1:26,27; James 3:9; Lev. 19:18; Luke 6:27,35; James 2:14-26; John 3:3,5; Matt. 5:20; 6:33; 2 Cor. 3:18; James 2:20)

6. THE CHURCH AND EVANGELISM

We affirm that Christ sends his redeemed people into the world as the Father sent him, and that this calls for a similar deep and costly penetration of the world. We need to break out of our ecclesiastical ghettos and permeate non-Christian society. In the Church's mission of sacrificial service evangelism is primary. World evangelization requires the whole Church to take the whole gospel to the whole world. The Church is at the very center of God's cosmic purpose and is his appointed means of spreading the gospel. But a church which preaches the cross must itself be marked by the cross. It becomes a stumbling block to evangelism when it betrays the gospel or lacks a living faith in God, a genuine love for people, or scrupulous honesty in all things including promotion and finance. The church is the community of God's people rather than an institution, and must not be identified with any particular cultural, social or political system, or human ideology. (John 17:18; 20:21; Matt. 28:19, 20; Acts 1:8; 20:27; Eph. 1:9,10; 3:9-11; Gal. 6:14,17; 2 Cor. 6:3, 4; 2 Tim. 2:19-21; Phil. 1:27)

7. COOPERATION IN EVANGELISM

We affirm that the Church's visible unity in truth is God's purpose. Evangelism also summons us to unity, because our oneness strengthens our witness, just as our disunity undermines our gospel of reconciliation. We recognize, however, that organizational unity may take many forms and does not necessarily forward evangelism. Yet we who share the same biblical faith should be closely united in fellowship, work and witness. We confess that our testimony has sometimes been marred by a sinful individualism and needless duplication. We pledge ourselves to seek a deeper unity in truth, worship, holiness and mission. We urge the development of regional and functional cooperation for the furtherance of the Church's mission, for strategic planning, for mutual encouragement, and for the sharing of resources and experience.
(John 17:21,23; Eph. 4:3,4; John 13:35; Phil. 1:27; John 17:11-23)

8. CHURCHES IN EVANGELISTIC PARTNERSHIP

We rejoice that a new missionary era has dawned. The dominant role of Western missions is fast disappearing. God is raising up from the younger churches a great new resource for world evangelization, and is thus demonstrating that the responsibility to evangelize belongs to the whole body of Christ. All churches should therefore be asking God and themselves what they should be doing both to reach their own area and to send missionaries to other parts of the world. A reevaluation of our missionary responsibility and role should be continuous. Thus a growing partnership of churches will develop and the universal character of Christ's Church will be more clearly exhibited. We also thank God for agencies which labor in Bible translation, theological education, the mass media, Christian literature, evangelism, missions, church renewal and other specialist fields. They too should engage in constant self-examination to evaluate their effectiveness as part of the Church's mission. (Rom. 1:8; Phil. 1:5; 4:15; Acts 13:1-3; 1 Thess. 1:6-8)

9. THE URGENCY OF THE EVANGELISTIC TASK

More than 2.7 billion people, which is more than two-thirds of all humanity, have yet to be evangelized. We are ashamed that so many have been neglected; it is a standing rebuke to us and to the whole Church. There is now, however, in many parts of the world an unprecedented receptivity to the Lord Jesus Christ. We are convinced that this is the time for churches and para-church agencies to pray earnestly for the salvation of the unreached and to launch new efforts to achieve world evangelization. A reduction of foreign missionaries and money in an evangelized country may sometimes be necessary to facilitate the national church's growth in self-reliance and to release resources for unevangelized areas. Missionaries should flow ever more freely from and to all six continents in a spirit of humble service. The goal should be, by all available means and at the earliest possible time, that every person will have the opportunity to hear, understand, and to receive the good news. We cannot hope to attain this goal without sacrifice. All of us are shocked by the poverty

of millions and disturbed by the injustices which cause it. Those of us who live in affluent circumstances accept our duty to develop a simple life-style in order to contribute more generously to both relief and evangelism.
(John 9:4; Matt. 9:35-38; Rom. 9:1-3; 1 Cor. 9:19-23; Mark 16:15; Isa. 58:6,7; James 1:27; 2:1-9; Matt. 25:31-46; Acts 2:44,45; 4:34,35)

10. EVANGELISM AND CULTURE

The development of strategies for world evangelization calls for imaginative pioneering methods. Under God, the result will be the rise of churches deeply rooted in Christ and closely related to their culture. Culture must always be tested and judged by Scripture. Because men and women are God's creatures, some of their culture is rich in beauty and goodness. Because they are fallen, all of it is tainted with sin and some of it is demonic. The gospel does not presuppose the superiority of any culture to another, but evaluates all cultures according to its own criteria of truth and righteousness, and insists on moral absolutes in every culture. Missions have all too frequently exported with the gospel an alien culture and churches have sometimes been in bondage to culture rather than to Scripture. Christ's evangelists must humbly seek to empty themselves of all but their personal authenticity in order to become the servants of others, and churches must seek to transform and enrich culture, all for the glory of God.
(Mark 7:8,9,13; Gen. 4:21,22; 1 Cor. 9:19-23; Phil. 2:5-7; 2 Cor. 4:5)

11. EDUCATION AND LEADERSHIP

We confess that we have sometimes pursued church growth at the expense of church depth, and divorced evangelism from Christian nurture. We also acknowledge that some of our missions have been too slow to equip and encourage national leaders to assume their rightful responsibilities. Yet we are committed to indigenous principles, and long that every church will have national leaders who manifest a Christian style of leadership in terms not of domination but of service.

We recognize that there is a great need to improve theological education, especially for church leaders. In every nation and culture there should be an effective training program for pastors and laity in doctrine, discipleship, evangelism, nurture and service. Such training programs should not rely on any stereotyped methodology but should be developed by creative local initiatives according to biblical standards.
(Col. 1:27,28; Acts 14:23; Titus 1:5,9; Mark 10:42-45; Eph. 4:11,12)

12. SPIRITUAL CONFLICT

We believe that we are engaged in constant spiritual warfare with the principalities and powers of evil, who are seeking to overthrow the Church and frustrate its task of world evangelization. We know our need to equip ourselves with God's armor and to fight this battle with the spiritual weapons of truth and prayer. For we detect the activity of our enemy, not only in false ideologies outside the church, but also inside it in false gospels which twist Scripture and put people in the place of God. We need both watchfulness and discernment to safeguard the biblical gospel. We acknowledge that we ourselves are not immune to worldliness of thought and actions, that is, to a surrender to secularism. For example, although careful studies of church growth, both numerical and spiritual, are right and valuable, we have compromised our message, manipulated our hearers through pressure techniques, and become unduly preoccupied with statistics or even dishonest in our use of them. All this is worldly. The Church must be in the world; the world must not be in the Church.
(Eph. 6:12; 2 Cor. 4:3,4; Eph. 6:11,13-18; 2 Cor. 10:3-5; 1 John 2:18-26; 4:1-3; Gal 1:6-9; 2 Cor. 2:17; John 17:15)

13. FREEDOM AND PERSECUTION

It is the God-appointed duty of every government to secure conditions of peace, justice and liberty in which the Church may obey God, serve the Lord Jesus Christ, and preach the gospel without interference. We therefore pray for the leaders of

nations and call upon them to guarantee freedom of thought and conscience, and freedom to practice and propagate religion in accordance with the will of God as set forth in The Universal Declaration of Human Rights. We also express our deep concern for all who have been unjustly imprisoned, and especially for those who are suffering for their testimony to the Lord Jesus. We promise to pray and work for their freedom. At the same time we refuse to be intimidated by their fate. God helping us, we too will seek to stand against injustice and to remain faithful to the gospel, whatever the cost. We do not forget the warnings of Jesus that persecution is inevitable.
(1 Tim. 1:1-4; Acts 4:19; 5:29; Col. 3:24; Heb. 13:1-3; Luke 4:18; Gal. 5:11; 6:12; Matt. 5:10-12; John 15:18-21)

14. THE POWER OF THE HOLY SPIRIT

We believe in the power of the Holy Spirit. The Father sent his Spirit to bear witness to his Son; without his witness ours is futile. Conviction of sin, faith in Christ, new birth and Christian growth are all his work. Further, the Holy Spirit is a missionary spirit; thus evangelism should arise spontaneously from a Spirit-filled church. A church that is not a missionary church is contradicting itself and quenching the Spirit. Worldwide evangelization will become a realistic possibility only when the Spirit renews the Church in truth and wisdom, faith, holiness, love and power. We therefore call upon all Christians to pray for such a visitation of the sovereign Spirit of God that all his fruit may appear in all his people and that all his gifts may enrich the body of Christ. Only then will the whole world become a fit instrument in his hands, that the whole earth may hear his voice.
(1 Cor. 2:4; John 15:26,27; 16:8-11; 1 Cor. 12:3; John 3:6-8; 2 Cor. 3:18; John 7:37-39; 1 Thess. 5:19; Acts 1:8; Ps. 85:4-7; 67:1-3; Gal. 5:22,23; 1 Cor. 12:4-31; Rom. 12:3-8)

15. THE RETURN OF CHRIST

We believe that Jesus Christ will return personally and visibly, in power and glory, to consummate his salvation and his

judgment. This promise of his coming is a further spur to our evangelism, for we remember his words that the gospel must first be preached to all nations. We believe that the interim period between Christ's ascension and return is to be filled with the mission of the people of God, who have no liberty to stop before the end. We also remember his warning that false Christs and false prophets will arise as precursors of the final Antichrist. We therefore reject as a proud, self-confident dream the notion that people can ever build a utopia on earth. Our Christian confidence is that God will perfect his kingdom, and we look forward with eager anticipation to that day, and to the new heaven and earth in which righteousness will dwell and God will reign forever. Meanwhile, we rededicate ourselves to the service of Christ and of people in joyful submission to his authority over the whole of our lives.
(Mark 14:62; Heb. 9:28; Mark 13:10; Acts 1:8-11; Matt. 28:20; Mark 13:21-23; John 2:18; 4:1-3; Luke 12:32; Rev. 21:1-5; 2 Peter 3:13: Matt. 28:18)

CONCLUSION

Therefore, in the light of this our faith and our resolve, we enter into a solemn covenant with God and with each other, to pray, to plan and to work together for the evangelization of the whole world. We call upon others to join us. May God help us by his grace and for his glory to be faithful to this our covenant! Amen, Alleluia!

Bibliography

Augustine, *City of God*.

Bettenson, Henry. *The Early Christian Fathers*. Oxford University Press, Oxford, 1956.

Boosahda, Wayne and Sly, Randy. "The Convergence Movement" article, written for *Twenty Centuries of Christian Worship*, by Dr. Robert Webber, ed.

Bruce, A.B. *The Training of the Twelve*, Copyright 1971, by Kregel Publications, a division of Kregel Inc., Grand Rapids, Michigan. Reproduced from the Fourth Edition, Revised and Improved, 1894, by A.C. Armstrong and Son.

Cunningham, William. *Historical Theology*. The Bath Press, Avon, Scotland, 1862.

Fee, Gordon D. *God's Empowering Presence*. Hendrickson Publishers, Inc., Peabody, Massachusetts, 1994.

Fee, Gordon D. *Paul, the Spirit, and the People of God*. Hendrickson Publishers, Inc., Peabody, Massachusetts, 1996.

Foster, Richard J. *Streams of Living Water*. HarperCollins Publishers, San Francisco, 1998.

George, Timothy. *Theology of the Reformers*. Broadman Press, Nashville, Tennessee, 1988.

Haggard, Ted. *The Life Giving Church*. Regal Books, Ventura California, 1998.

Hayes, Ed L. *The Church*. Word Publishing, Nashville, Tennessee, 1999.

Hester, H.I. *The Heart of Hebrew History*. Broadman Press, Nashville, Tennessee, 1949.

Hill, Andrew E. *Enter His Courts with Praise*. Baker Books, Grand Rapids, Michigan, 1993.

Mendelson, Jonathan and Blumenthal, Elana. A paper titled "Chaos Theory and Fractals."

Merriam-Webster's Collegiate Dictionary, Tenth Edition, 1995, published by Merriam-Webster Incorporated.

Moore, Peter C. *A Church to Believe In*. Latimer Press, Bainbridge, Ohio, 1994.

Newbigin, Lesslie. *The Household of God*. Paternoster Press, London, first published 1953 (SCM Press Ltd.), reprinted 1998.

Norris, Jr., Richard A. "Bishops, Succession, and the Apostolicity of the Church," published as a chapter in *On Being a Bishop*. The Church Hymnal Corporation, New York, 1993.

Rupp, E. Gordon, "Christian Doctrine from 1350 to the Eve of the Reformation," *A History of Christian Doctrine*. Hubert Cunliffe-Jones, ed. (Edinburg: T. and T. Clark, 1978). John Wycliffe. *English Works*. F. D. Matthew, ed. (London: Trubner and Co., 1880).

Sanders, John Oswald. *Spiritual Leadership*. Moody Press, Chicago, 1902, 1967, 1980.

Shelley, Bruce L. *Church History in Plain Language*. Word Publishing, Dallas, Texas, 1982, 1985.

Shibley, David. *A Force in the Earth*. Creation House, Orlando, Florida, 1989, 1997.

The Book of Common Prayer, Church Hymnal Corporation, New York.

Synan, Vinson. *The Century of the Holy Spirit: 100 Years of Pentecostal and Charismatic Renewal, 1901-2001*. Thomas Nelson Inc., Nashville, Tennessee, 2001.

The Chicago-Lambeth Quadrilateral 1886, 1888.

Tozer, A. W. "The Use and Abuse of Books" article written for *Alliance Weekly,* February 22, 1956, p. 2.

Wagner, C. Peter, *The New Apostolic Churches*. Regal Books, Ventura, California, 1998.

Warren, Rick. *The Purpose Driven Church*. Zondervan Corporation, Grand Rapids, Michigan, 1995.

Webber, Robert E. *Ancient-Future Faith*. Baker Books, Grand Rapids, Michigan, 1999.

Webber, Robert E. *Evangelicals on the Canterbury Trail*. Morehouse Publishing, Harrisburg, Pennsylvania, 1985.

Wright, J. Robert. The Ministry of Bishops: A Study Document Authorized by The House of Bishops of the Episcopal Church. Published by Trinity Institute, Trinity Parish, New York, 1991.

The Sound of Rushing Waters
Order Form

Postal orders: Dquest Group
P.O. Box 52
Ponte Vedra Beach, FL
32004-0052

Telephone orders: 904-285-3308

E-mail orders: dquestgroup@yahoo.com

Website orders: www.dquestgroup.com

Please send *The Sound of Rushing Waters* to:

Name: _____

Address: _____

City: _____ State: _____

Zip: _____ Telephone: (_____) _____

Book Price: $15.95

Shipping: $3.00 for the first book and $1.00 for each additional book to cover shipping and handling within US, Canada, and Mexico.
International orders add $6.00 for the first book and $2.00 for each additional book.

or contact your local bookstore

911 Promise
by Daniel Williams

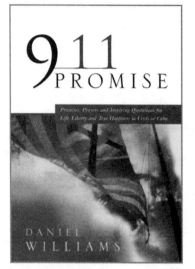

ISBN: 0884199274

"Finding God's promises no matter what the circumstance"

A remarkable response to the events of September 11. Here is a God-honoring, flag-flying, awe-inspiring presentation by Dr. Daniel Williams that will help our nation look up and get the big picture. Various passages of Scripture with an amazing correlation to 9/11, dynamic quotations from American patriots and passionate prayers are woven together with stirring narrative. Dr. Williams sets the stage with a poignant quote from Dr. Martin Luther King: "Our scientific power has outrun our spiritual power. We have guided missiles and misguided men." From there, he launches into a thought-provoking chapter entitled "A Promise of Protection" using Genesis 9:11 as the biblical reference. Regarding this work, Williams shares, "Every day across America, people in emergency situations of life call 911. However, it is important that we know whom to call. Let us never neglect to call upon God's Word for help." Every chapter offers hope and encouragement and challenges Americans to keep a strong faith for the days ahead.

Destiny Quest Publications
A Division of Dquest Group, Incorporated
P.O. Box 52
Ponte Vedra Beach, Florida 32004-0052

Also available at your local Christian bookstore

**For more information and free resources visit
www.dquestgroup.com**